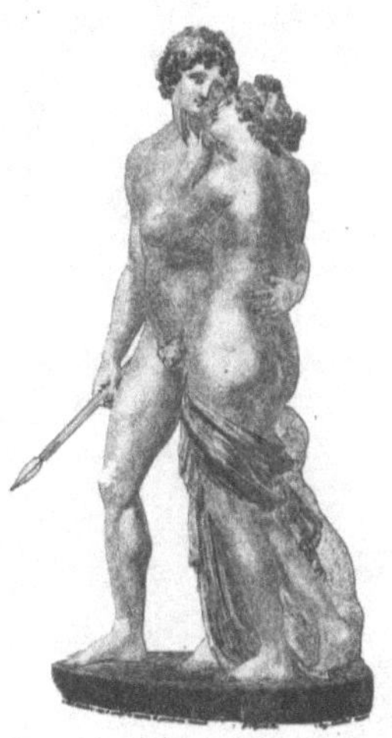

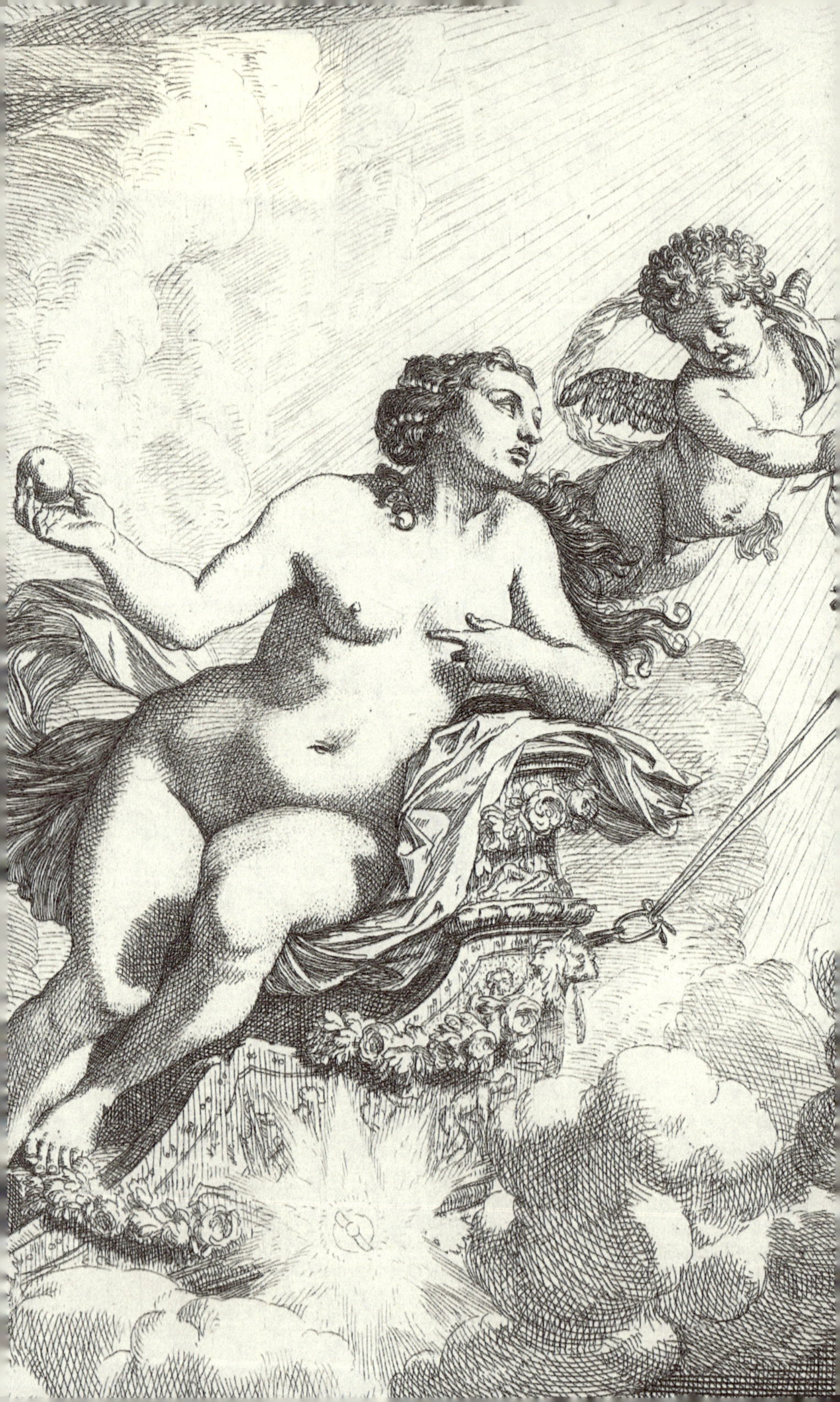

Scarlett Gray
presents

Venus Reborn

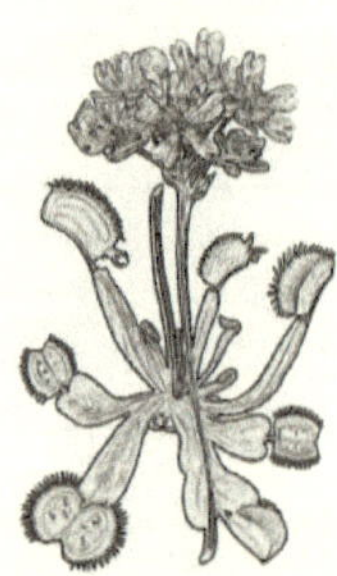

Photographs by Pierre Krause:
back cover portrait and film stills on page 94
All other photographs by Scarlett Gray
Public Domain artwork courtesy of Europeana Collections
"Gay in California" first appeared in *Peach Fuzz Magazine,* June 2020

ISBN 978-0-578-64678-7

Preface: the Birth of *Venus Reborn*

[September, 2019] It's six a.m. I'm in L.A. for the first time in years, visiting a friend whom I credit with helping to drastically change my life for the better a year and a half ago. It's late September, Virgo season in full swing, everything a mess of organized chaos. At the stroke of midnight, it became my coworker's birthday. They're here with me in California, sharing the pale pink living room of this cozy and glamorous West Hollywood apartment. I've woken up early to sit in the cold blast of the air conditioner, watch the sun first touch the room, and write poetry in the comforting haze of early-morning sleepiness combined with the tail-end of bedtime edibles.

Life always seems it has more to offer me when I'm away from home. I've chased the color sea foam green, let it reveal itself to me as a sign that I'm where I'm meant to be. The air feels fresher out on the West Coast, even though this city seems to be constantly on fire. I feel woven in here, so much more seamlessly than in the city I've lived my entire life. I understand why so many legends cling to the iconography, the immortality of everyone who lived and died here. You can feel the ghosts of so many beautiful, mistreated women wailing in the wind; of so many evil men who got away with too much, laughing from the afterlife, of so many others just figuring it out along the way. It might not be real, but I can feel it.

I've tried to stop writing so much about ghosts, to let them go so they can't continue to haunt me within my own work, but maybe sometimes that's how you release them. I go back and forth, wondering whether writing about people in my past gives them power over me, or me over them, or maybe it really makes no difference in the long run.

My friends have a theory that Los Angeles is purgatory. In some way, I think that's what I like about it. Time stands more still, and is somehow both harder and easier to keep track of. No amount of iced coffee seems like too much, and restaurants serve healthy versions of our childhood comfort foods. Everyone is someone and everyone is no one. People drive like they're trying to win a video game, like if you crash you just have to restart whatever level you're on. As if there aren't any real stakes. I eat it up, really—that indescribable feeling of "*yeah, maybe I could really be somebody someplace like this.*" You know?

[March, 2020] In 2018 I became obsessed with the idea of Venus—the goddess, the planet, the small town thirty minutes south of my home (where they filmed some of *Bonnie and Clyde*, and it still somewhat looks like an old film set). I feel such a strong connection to her, this ruling planet of my earthy sun sign and airy ascendant, this personification of all things fertile. My writing began to hover back and forth between poems about the state of the world—the terrifying people in positions of power—and the rebirth of my sexuality. In late 2019, the synchronicities between myself and my love of Venus started fully revealing themselves to me. I baptized myself at the shoreline of Latigo Beach, tattooed Venus on my hand, and entered into an artistic venture creating adult content under the pseudonym *Venus*.

The older I get, the more I have to try to cope with the thought that, in my lifetime, sex work may not be seen as an acceptable source of income, a career, or an art form by the general public. Politicians continue to fight against our existence with legislation like SESTA/FOSTA that directly harm sex workers. Celebrities push projects that claim to tell our stories, but in reality, further solidify the same old tired tropes while shooting on location, causing strip clubs to close down and workers to lose wages.

People who've seen censored previews of my premium content have asked why I consider myself a sex worker, trying to compliment me by telling me that, to them, I'm an artist. And while I know the intentions are good, I'll keep screaming until I can't anymore that the two aren't mutually exclusive, and that one isn't better or more noble than the other. Being a dancer when I was eighteen was no more demeaning than the minimum-wage grocery store job I worked a year prior to that. And while I use an artistic eye in every post I make on OnlyFans, sex work doesn't have to be artistic in order for it to be valid. If any of this sounds strange to you or feels hard to grasp, I urge you to open your mind and unlearn any prejudices you may be holding against sex workers.

I'd like to dedicate this book to each of the people who made it possible, by making my existence brighter in different but equally-important ways. To Mom and Aaron, for never asking me to change, and for supporting me even when you don't understand (p.s. sorry for the nudity). To Carlos and Austin (and Stove), for letting me seek refuge with y'all in Los Angeles. To Pierre and Misael, for keeping me sane and always having my back. Y'all truly are my ride-or-dies. To Karen and Erica, for all the beauty you've given me. I'm sorry I'm so bad at staying in touch. To Azra and Georgina, for always lending a loving ear. To the other poets, artists, and beautiful beings who encouraged and inspired me. To all the Main Street kids who cried with me during work hours (or gave me free coffee when I was crying during work hours). That old-world shit still hits in my heart. To Dr. Sapp, wherever you are, for believing in me when no one else did. To all my lovers, past, present, and future—anyone who ever touched me in a way that didn't hurt.

All my love,
Scarlett/Venus

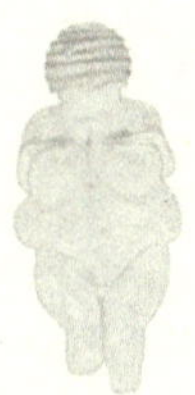

ACT I

ACT II

INTERMISSION:

ACT III

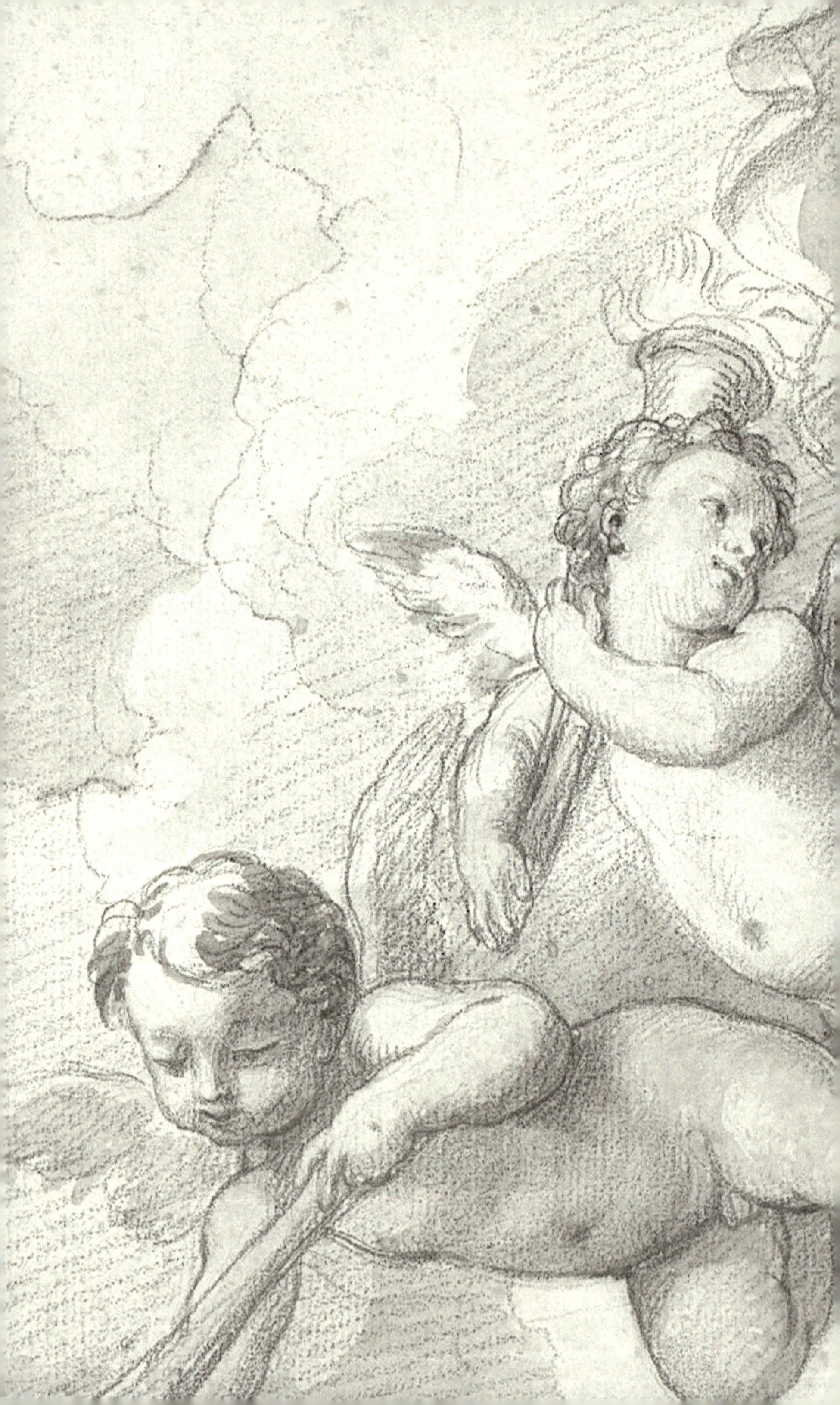

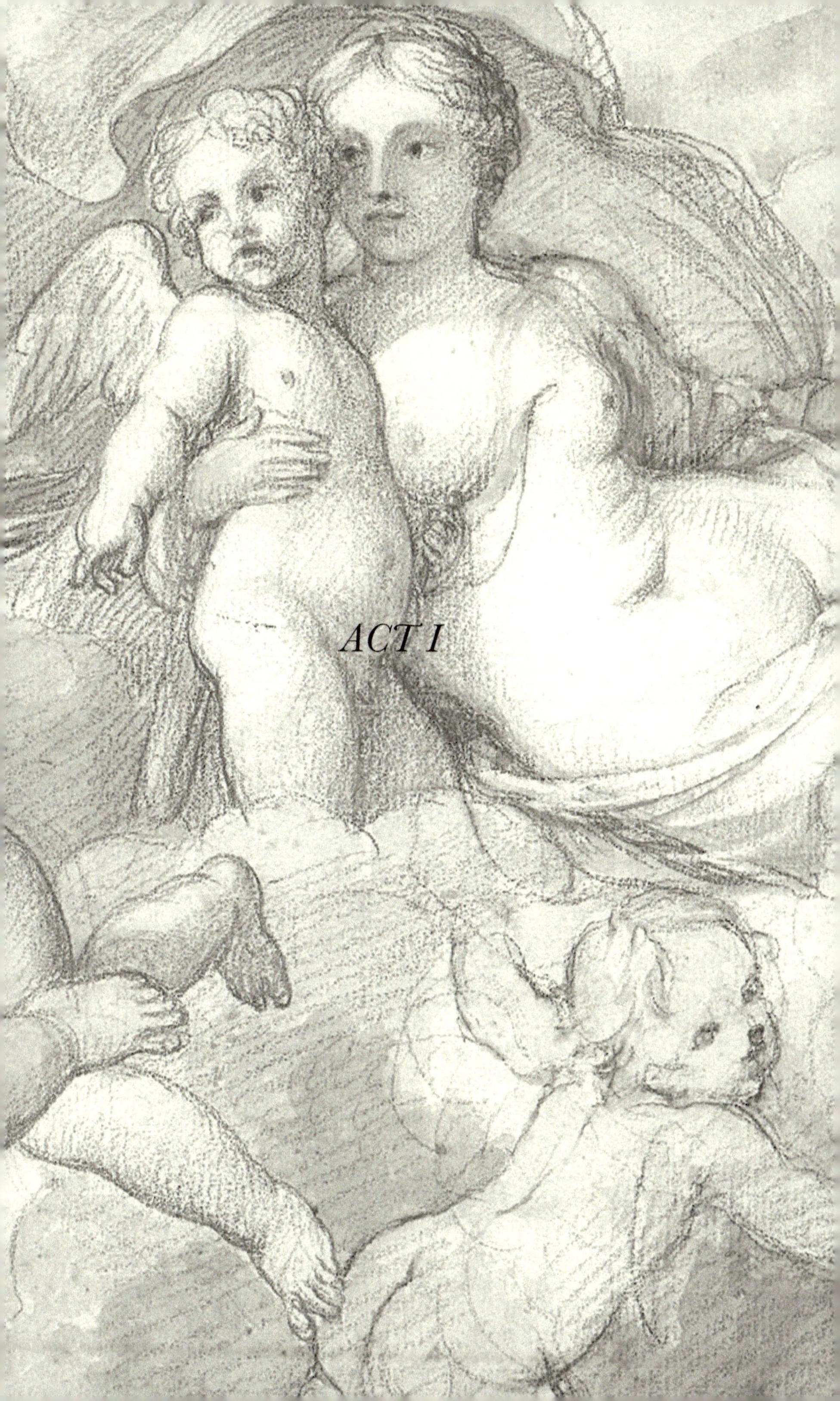

ACT I

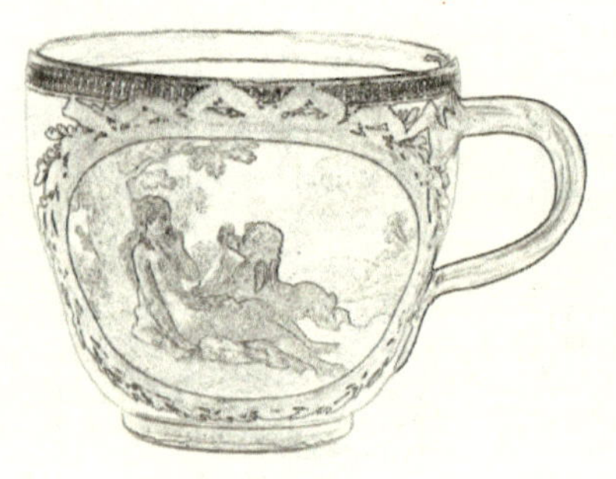

Microcosm

And so, the sirens sing, sunrise on into imminent darkness, immortalized sensations of danger overshadowed beyond recognition in a mid-tempo trance engulfing us in the relentless, anesthetizing bullshit of tactile transgressions and their creators, marking time, waiting in the wings to inherit the earth by any means, dead or alive, overflowing or on fire like the state of California—Manson tries to drag her down to hell with him; oh, she is resilient

9 to 5

I boil with the Texas summer, hotheaded
    wearing hair so blonde it burns

The lining of my blazer sticks to my bare skin,
    my face dewy with sweat by every afternoon

The sizzling asphalt smells
    like feverish road trips to nowhere

What might it be like to melt away
    into the cracks in the pavement?

I sign in, clock in,
    get into character and sell what I'm asked to—

Diamonds, lap dances,
    books filled with big dicks or bigger architecture

$400 serums
    and Gwyneth Paltrow's rose quartz vagina eggs

Strangers stand in the corner of the shop,
    flip open my younger face
        and read about all the boys who ever hurt me

Their eyes skim over the things
    I won't even let my mother read

I lose a staring contest with the sculpture across the street,
        blinking as construction kicks up dust into the air

That giant fucking blue eye
        looking back at me doesn't flinch

I shed a tear for the both of us

I entertain! The doll of Downtown Dallas,
        performance artist of the retail hours
                permanently hung-over on 9-to-5ing

The wallpaper is peeling apart
        on purpose

I'm sure I've swallowed a few flies

My voice grows more southern
        with every tourist encounter

I dabble with *y'all*
        until it becomes a sincere part of me

I oversleep

My skin smells like depression
        masked beneath too many layers
                of soft jasmine and ylang ylang
                        and I eat cereal standing up to feel like a kid again

Do my pulse points smell happy now?
        My neck tastes like serotonin
                I become a giant Prozac with a dry mouth

I listen to podcasts on ethical consumerism
        Both my bosses bought my book on Amazon

I have the words, *How are you today*?
        permanently trapped on my taste buds

Hollow and insincere, empty calories
        for mass consumption

The flowers we sell are already dead

Today is taking forever
I stew for six hours, but outside it's only two
Time was never real, anyway

My boss and I text poems across the block,
selling erotica while writing about our sex lives

It's Pride Week and we're both fucking men
I feel like a fraud

I draw a sloppy Texas on my arm in green pen,
write haikus about a flowering cactus

Drown in the mirror, chew gum instead of food,
whisper minty poems into my phone
and text them out to their inspirers

I gently touch every object of the shop
and let them touch me back,

A mist of perfume and oils
and glass bottles glistening in the sun

In the nighttime, I shy away
from the people who care about me
and let straight girls kiss me
when they want to feel wild

I'm a toy, a prop,
another object to be played with

I'm still sad in the morning
What does either of us gain?

In the day, I'm a number,
an employee ID, a sales record

I stay in place, tread water
and work harder than I'm paid to

My arms grow tired,
it becomes hard to breathe

Is this what drowning feels like?

I switch from contacts to glasses
so I'll be taken more seriously

I must've forgotten these things never work

My blood, sweat, and tears
line the lobby of this building

What do I have to do for you to see me?

If I pull my hair back into a tight, tidy bun
and shove my tits into a firm sports bra...

If I wear long pants and squeeze my toes
into clicking black kitten heels...

If I never question incompetence above me
and shut my mouth after saying only *yes*...

Then will I be enough?

I'm still learning
to choose anger over sadness

Someone told me sad girls
don't get to move up the ladder

A clementine rots on top of the mini fridge
A mosquito bites my ankle
The summers always taste like blood

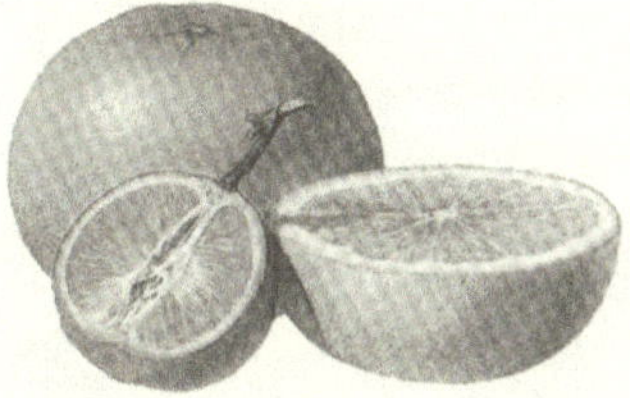

Itch

Instagram went down and I forgot what I look like,
Forget that small limelight, your mirrors
Aren't as forgiving as a curated grid

How do I move my body?
How do I stand still?

Summer melts the colors off my face,
Exposes thin lips, tired under-eyes,
Sweat-clogged pores and smeared mascara

Who am I without likes?
Will I slide off the planet Earth?
Sink into the depths of inexistence?

I make myself smaller,
More mutable, less sharp
And with a tongue free of venom

I hide the plumper parts of me,
Let long bangs act as curtains over my face,
Soften my voice so I feel like a girl

Fuck it!
You can see me when I'm ugly

I climb on top of you in the kitchen, beg you
To be rough with me
But wince when you love me
Like I'm fragile

I give you my body as freely as I'm able
Until the novelty of my newness rubs off

Do you still love me
When I dry up?

Double tap my clitoris, comment on my ass
Rate review and subscribe to our sex acts

You call me your angel, I don't want to feel holy
Spit your love back into your mouth
I know you're afraid I'll break

Maybe I'm mistaking roughness with passion
Stealing your sleep, indulging the night
By praying to be loved
So hard it hurts me

All my exes got married
Blowjobs still taste like rape
I think people forget that healing will itch

Peach Iced Tea

gentle growth once turned violent against timid actions
sparking artificially-sweetened summers,
lilac lemonade heavy in my throat
like explorations in identity
and your love withheld
in the name of heavenly transformation

and communal searches for salvation
or what salvation really means, but only for you
the answers taking up unfamiliar spaces
in my head

spare me your speeches
I am whole without you

so why do I still want to follow you astray? to the space
in which man thinks he becomes prophet
and every other being is nothing more than a reflection
of his self,
a watery mirror existing only to orbit him
and teach the lessons he so craves to learn

cycles run unbroken
from heavily self-medicated minds

have you seen too much?
the sickening intricacies of craving pain
but only on my own terms

electric afternoons I can't piece together
billowing skirts and curtains in the wind
chemistry
my love
so underestimated

it took me two years
but I learned forgiveness in my sleep,
closure behind my eyelids
trickles into the day

I am new to this world
passing the time with past bad habits I kicked
and came crawling back to
on my hands and knees, begging please

resistant to living beneath invisible veils
someplace nearer than here
I am not welcome with you

the culture of youth
embedded in the downtown scene
popping pills and piles of poppers,
wholesome choreo on the Round Up dance floor
tempting me to let my hair down,
to begin again

sweet love in the corner,
take the breath straight from my lungs,
the words from my mouth,
the hours from my memory

take the pain from my mind,
another kind of poison

just flick your fucking cigarette
and get me out of here

but our clocks are all melting
and so too, hell is a place on earth
sharing custody with heaven,
hands tugging on each arm

we don't get to pick our parents

the Great American Sapphic Love Poem

The sea is calm

(They say you find peace in your final moments)

In over my head, another kind of womb
Submerged in the earth's amniotic fluid

Venus in my blood,
Her temperament
Pulling out all the stops

What was it you once said?
That I was holding my breath,
Waiting for someone to give me permission?

Hearts beat behind the ears,
The soft *whoosh*ing pulse of satisfying fear

Can't even look you in the eyes
Sneaking glances like trying to stare at the sun

Hoping you'll notice, praying you won't
My shyness only knows true love in the dark

But I'd stare into the sun if you said it could heal me,
Let her take my vision in exchange for something better

Let us be better

If you let me take my sweet time
I can be your mother nature

And you mine,
The girls with the hand tattoos
Rubbing off on one another

Love me soft
And rough and gentle

I'll let you pretend
To be in control

Fuck me until I'm dumb
A cute idiot with flushed cheeks and swollen lips,
Ecstasy and an empty brain

Screaming out the great American sapphic love poem
Between breaths

(Wash my mouth out with soap if I'm saying too much)

Teetering between sex and politics,
The end of the world and the end of an orgasm,
Injustice and gestation,
All the things Venus can feel at her core—

My offering to you
Placed at the altar that is your self,
Soul and body,
Texas roses and barbed wire

Love me through my writing,
Through these thoughts
I never said aloud

Arguments we never had
But I worked through, here, instead

Love me through the mad,
Through the darkness that sometimes
Seems will never end,
Through those times I get mean and manic
And say things without thinking

And let me love you when you're selfish
And absent and inattentive

When I can tell that you're angry
But you don't want to talk, anymore

When you withhold without meaning to,
Let me love you

Kiss me until I can feel it
Through all my past lives,
Touching every body in which I've ever lived

Tempt me toward permanence,
Toward unspoken vows held in the air between us

Whisper words I'll remember in the morning
I can only breathe if you can see me

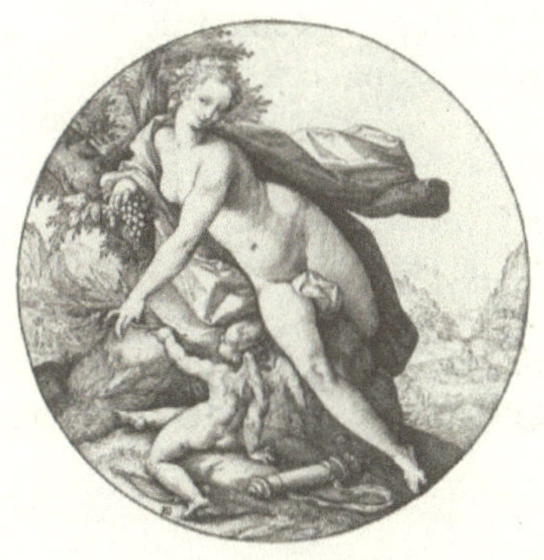

Gay in California

I left my love in the Hollywood hills
And watched the palm trees droop behind her
I guess I forgot again, things can wilt anywhere
No city is Eden, no garden green enough to heal us

My sense of euphoria was swept away
With the Santa Ana winds,
Fanning flames and leaving lamenting lovers in her wake,
Forgotten dreams within a dreamland
Illusory images fade to black on a soundstage

I lost my ring at LAX
And watched the TSA agents, all blue gloves and bravado,
Perform their choreographed dance
For the stressed and sleepy, the hopeful and heartbroken
In a single file line snaking around the room

The sun is rising in Santa Monica
But it's gray and frozen in Texas,
Slick highways lined with crumpled cars,
Flashing lights every five miles
Of the deadly Dallas freeway

In my better dreams, I'm back in California
Wearing your necklace, waiting for you to come home
To your home,
To *our* home

Bury my broken heart beneath Mulholland Drive,
And I'll be afraid to drive down it
For more than one reason,
Memories lined into each small crack in the pavement
Of paradise

The girl I loved was a little devil on my shoulder
With an angel's face, dressed in all red,
Translating every language from fact to temptation
From fear to adrenaline
From risk to reward

The girl I loved was a sacred heart
Beating too fast to hear, spilling blood
Across state lines, a darkened route through the map
From Texas to California

I left my love above the Hollywood sign
And on the Malibu Pier
And Top of Topanga Overlook

Maybe someday the sun will bleach into my skull,
Erase the colors of my mind
So that I don't miss her as much

Take me back to the maddening L.A. traffic
To the oat milk Spanish lattes
            served up cold at the drive-in
To the stone fruits we left submerged in the sand
To the brief pockets of accidental scientology
To the beautiful and the bad
            and the graveyards of good and evil

I just want
To go back and be
Gay in California

Earthy

recovery has many entrances, but humanity remains, stewing in the din of what our countless medications and alternative methods of healing can't cure, tuned-in to the hostile frequencies sent out to each of us, laced in earth-shattering error warnings—messages about leaving punctured earthly flesh for brighter homes in apparent heavens abandoned by the gods upon hearing rumors of sweeter paradise, higher up above theirs

we gloss over these messages—loud and shiny, but too soft, too concealed to overpower all of the madness coming at us from every angle

and what will we leave behind? what we can't erase—the earthy taste on our tongues, absent from all that we've touched and left destructive marks on, compromised by gluttonous fights for power and control of nature, who does not take well to being controlled

do we set her on fire? or does she, herself burst into flames—a desperate, suicidal act meant to express her last frantic ultimatum, and so warmly received by mankind with futility? do we even attempt to save her?

the smells of both smoke and wet grass linger in the air; incessant decisive storms leave no reprieve, no room for exhaling bated breaths in exchange for fresher air in early November when there's a chance for change

this is where we deliberately retreat, folding into the widening cracks in the dirt, and down deeper into our home and our earthly delights, our precious possessions caving in on us until we're reduced down to fossilized souvenirs for Mother Earth, infant reminders of what we've done to her

this is what we've built—a gasping nest unable to sustain itself unless we're willing to change

how do we leave our bodies, shed the skin we've worn out and marked with the things that mean the most to us, and transcend onto the next paradise, which we'll inevitably strip dry, feeding off of until we've left an empty vessel, much like our past selves?

is life wasted on us? has all of this been an exit strategy? sabotaging the things around us like petulant children not getting their way? existence—a tantrum, leaving us waiting to see if anyone calls our bluff, so maddening for passive participators waiting out what might never end

or what might end all too quickly

a Dead Baby Bird with a Broken Neck

A dead baby bird with a broken neck,
canary yellow and alone,
lays at the corner of Main Street and Akard

A woman across the street
in a yellow tulle gown
and black platform high heels
spins in the wind for a camera
while construction workers in bright orange
watch her

The shutter blinks, closes and opens,
looks at its subject only briefly,
afraid to stare into her
as if she is blinding

The sun peaks out her head,
paints my blonde hair yellow
as I say a slight prayer
for the little bird

Babies are born in the spring

for Easter Sunday,
pastels and hungry cries
harmonize with old hymns in church services,
wedding ceremonies in suburbia

Los Angeles takes a tumble,
falls open and breaks its spine
on the floor of my bookshop,
vibrant sky blue
and falling apart

I can't hear anything over footsteps on loud floor—
black stilettos and brown boots sweeping their hosts from Main to Commerce—
tuning in as if, if I listen hard enough,
I can hear their direction
and beckon them toward me

The sun sets and sets
and sets as if I don't need her,
as if I haven't wept and begged her not to leave me
again

I wrap my arms around me,
hold my own body, rock back and forth gently for comfort
like holding warm tea, that moment your insides become honey
like holding an advance copy of a book, a special secret
like I wanted to hold that little bird, but I knew I couldn't
like rocking a baby to sooth her into sleep

Wake up!
A sore spinal cord in someone else's sack of flesh
morning breath in someone else's mouth
aches behind someone else's left eye
memories of someone else's regrets

I swallow pills,
drown them in an ocean of iced coffee
hoping they can help me

I up my dosage,
my happy pills evolve from purple
to bubble gum pink,

and I fight the urge to chew them
like sweet candy

Fight the urge to say
fuck it
and flush them away
(why not get it over with now?
before I lose my insurance
and can't afford to have depression)

A dead gray bird
lays stiff and alone
at the center of the parking lot
on the corner of Field and San Jacinto

Death, always at my feet
like when stray cats leave
tiny mouse skulls at the doorstep,
gruesome offerings

She just wanted to be a good girl
I came and went out the back door for days
because I couldn't bear it—
the crunch of baby bones, so many ants
in a single-file line

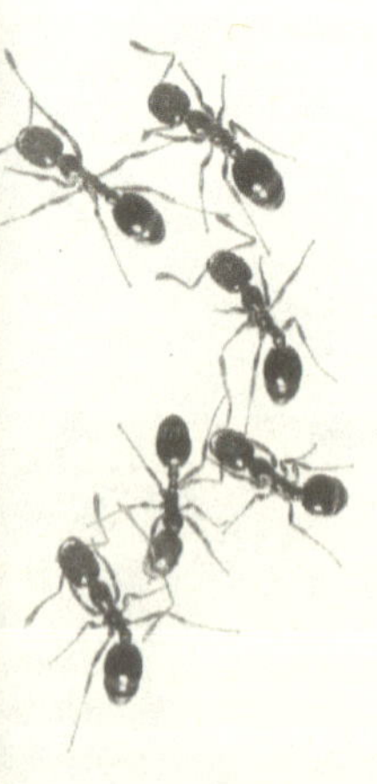

I Never Thought I'd Live to Be An Adult, So Forgive Me if I Have No Plan

When my growth needs to take a breath,
I put her on pause while I spiral
In the gentlest way possible

Ease in with bad first dates,
Blow off seconds

Let little white pills
Sing me to sleep

I drink when I run out
And don't flinch when men choke me

Does a broken part of me
Still want to be mistreated?

Self-harmful tendencies can only hide for so long
Rebelling against the things I need the very most

I'm so tired of tucking my traumas into bed,
Kissing them goodnight,
Wiping their tears in the dark,
Their regretful mother

Can't I go back to neglecting them,
Just for a minute?

I never thought I'd live to be an adult,
So forgive me if I have no plan

At 25, I etch these words into my arm
In green ink
Only to recoil when strangers try to talk to me about it
Three days later

I flip the pages of a large-scale book
For a woman who reads the flesh on my forearm instead,
Tells me her own tragic testimony like a performer
At the Christian concerts I went to as a child
(Cut the music for an awkward crowd therapy session
That ends in you all finding god)

I keep tracing my arm
Until the letters aren't raised anymore

The ink settles into my skin,
Healed before I am

I'm an open heart, a confessional,
Somewhere for strangers to place their problems
So that they can breathe again

I listen, nod my head and feel every word
Roll through me

I forget how to swallow
Past the lump in my throat,
Clench my jaw and hold back
Someone else's tears

And I want to be that person! That person who can
Observe everyone else's pain
Without feeling it, feeding it and giving it a home
In a way I know isn't helping either of us

I sit in bed and cry
Over some stranger's heartbreak,
That girl with the short hair's
(I can't remember her name)
Dying mother

I follow memories, guided by the hand
Back to days I can still hardly think about
When tender 25 felt too final and abstract
To ever imagine being

I never thought I'd live this long
Did I project it onto all of us?

I could've sworn we felt the same,
Like there would be nothing left
For us on earth after our teenage years

And that by some force—
Whether or own hand, someone else's,
Or an act of divine intervention—
We would disappear, remaining only as a memory
Of some hot, young, wannabe-artists who died too soon

Full of promise and potential, eating disorders
And self-inflicted wounds

I thought I was almost done

That I knew enough
And felt enough
And loved enough
And so brutally hurt enough
That the idea of a future was impossible

Nothing felt drastic, then, about the idea killing myself
If life didn't kill me first

I never thought I'd live to be an adult
But here we are, 26 and I still don't know
What the fuck I'm doing

I sit, refrigerated, alone in a cold room
Surrounded by books, some so expensive
My heart skips a beat when I turn pages
As performance art,
(This too fades with time;
Our white gloves are turning gray by the touch)

I move from shitty job to shitty job
To great but temporary job
To great job with abusive management
And never know what it feels like
To have my feet firmly on the ground

Do we ever get better? Or do our plagues and problems
Follow us forever, growing older with us,
Wiser with us, stronger with us?

I don't want any more EMDR
Maybe my brain just needs a break
From healing

The world is my new therapist
I tell my deepest fears to anyone who asks
And doesn't shy away

I regress—give myself bruises when other people don't
Care for myself ruthlessly, fueled by all my bad habits
And the damaging ways of coping
I unlearned for a few months
And then only slipped deeper into

A friend asks
Are you okay? Your voice is small today

I change my name to something sharper—Scarlett,
The "ka" and the "tt",
Harsh noises that feel so much better
In my mouth than what my parents named me

That little name I only hear in the suburbs south of Dallas
Where we used to practice dying
In preparation

I consume myself with sex until it becomes an obsession
And then learn to obsess over the concept of obsession,
Spending nights sleeping with people
Who give me attention in the way I crave it

Even though I *know* I want to feel desired

More than I want to gratify

We've been through this all before—
Wanting someone who'll worship me enough to hurt me
In the small ways I need to be hurt

To see me as shiny
And hot
And new

To love me in the desperate ways I need to be loved,
To feel the love I have nowhere to put down,
But can't hold onto anymore

Hurt me just enough,
But not so much I keep attaching being hurt
To being loved

Still, I live day-to-day, week-to-week,
Month-to-month in the best of times,
Minute-to-minute in the worst

I download the meditation apps,
Use them three times before giving up
Choose instead to find hope through crossing tasks off a list
Through sincere interactions
Through dancing at Sue Ellen's and Havana
On a Thursday night

I polish my résumé,
Catering to the unknown,
Highlighting skills that might not matter
In the long run,
Look over the pages
And wonder who I am

People ask me what I want to do
As if I'm supposed to have an answer,
As if I ever had the foresight
To think this far ahead

It's hard to strategize in long stretches of time
What's a five-year-plan

When you thought you'd be dead five years ago?

How do I learn to conceptualize a future
Further than finishing this goddamn book?

Am I buying myself more time
Because I fear when this is over
I'll only feel empty?

I don't know what's next
And the thought of that
Is all-consuming

Too terrifying to allow into my head
Just yet

So if you're reading this,
At least we can both say
We made it this far

Graduating Therapy

I spend my last therapy session silently reflecting
on how I became the girl who begs a man who loves me
to slap me in the face during sex

I haven't written in months, momentum is a stranger
I feel dumb and ugly and unremarkable

I'm still standing outside of parties,
and I still have to be high to orgasm from men
I don't tell my therapist any of this

I try to find my identity on the outside,
wear certain clothes to feel boyish or cloudlike,
let people think they know me through this performance
without ever a word exchanged between us

I itch with the urge to spend money I don't have—
an itch no amount of scratching
ever seems to satiate

What's another credit card
when debt feels so intangible?

I buy condoms, lube, and a candle
that melts to massage oil,
justifying so many purchases
with my employee discount
and using sex as my only means of validation,
trying to heal from the outside in

At the end of the day, I try to remember
what floor I'm parked on

Everything is heavy,
the air stings in my lungs

I've learned to hit *lock* as soon as I close the car door,
to quickly peek in my back windows while getting inside,
to walk with pepper spray always in my pocket,
to practice screaming so I remember that I can

I've learned to take deep breaths
before getting on the highway,
to notice the feeling of the wheel in my hands,
my foot heavy on the pedal

I've learned binging on comfort food
will only make me feel worse,
too bad the knowledge doesn't stop me

I eat a row of Oreo's as my only meal,
text a boy that I started my period
and I'm in bed wanting to die

He says, *Yay!* because it means I'm not pregnant
(I thought we already knew this)

I buy clothes in my sleep,
feel the chemical imbalance

I'm sleeping too much,
and I know what this leads to

When things are fine but I'm not,
there's nowhere concrete to attach my sadness

So I make things out to be bigger issues than they are
and staple my anxieties onto those pages,
whispering *this makes sense, now*

Giving it a name
even if the name doesn't fit

My (ex) therapist asks if it's time for she and I to break up
(not in those terms, but that's how I heard it)

Is this supposed to be
what progress feels like?

When I'm shy, she asks if I see her as a motherly figure
I don't ever tell her quite how deeply

She shows me line graphs, down and up
and down down down
and up
to show me how far I've come

Sometimes it's hard to remember
where we've been

Remember that old mantra?
I am worthy and deserving of love
I am worthy
and deserving
of love

As I leave, she hugs me, like she did
when I looked into her eyes
and promised I wouldn't kill myself
two years ago

She says
fly away, little bird. I'm proud of you

And I don't know how to feel

Girl

Men sometimes ask me why I say
It's just easier to be with women

As if letting men in
Doesn't come with risks and statistics

As if I've ever known a man
Who never crossed my boundaries without asking
Who never made me crawl in my skin

Who never made me wonder if I need to tell someone
Exactly where I am, just in case

As if my body doesn't know how easy it is to become
Just another dead girl

Muscle memory tells me I have no fight or flight,
I can only play dead

Boys weren't taught the same rules we were:

Don't walk alone at night
Or in the daytime

Don't make eye contact
But be aware of the men around you

If you think someone is following you, make random turns
To throw them off
Until you get somewhere bright and public

Let your girlfriends track your phone location
Everywhere you go

Send a drop pin,
Maybe save your life

Don't get drunk
Or leave a drink unattended

(They tried to make that nail polish that changes colors
If you dip it in a roofied drink, but are you really
Certain enough
To take a sip?)

Clutch your keys between your knuckles,
Only wear shoes you can run in

Short skirt? What a slut
Be classy
Dress conservative
Don't be a prude
Be sexy
Don't be a tease

Don't show too much skin,
Leave something to the imagination
Don't be so covered up,
Their imaginations will run wild

Get sent home from school if your shirt straps
Aren't at least three fingers wide,

Because how can you expect
Those sweet young boys to focus?

You'll corrupt them with that filthy flesh on your shoulders,
Every twelve-year-old girl must be some secret temptress

How many more times do I have to hear someone ask
Well, what was she wearing?
As if it's ever fucking mattered?

Buy a stun gun
But no, don't buy a stun gun
Because you have to get close to use it and they can
Grab it away from you
And use it against you
Use anything against you
Use everything against you

I can still hear my mother explaining to me at six or seven
Long hair is easier to grab

Don't get in an elevator with a man you don't know
(Or maybe even one you do)
Unless you want to end up on the 5 o'clock news

They won't even say your name
They'll call you "girl" or "wife" or "mother"

Pour one out for all the girls we never found
The girls whose bodies rot in hiding spots
The girls we never even looked for
Because they fucked for money,
Lived in "bad" neighborhoods,
Or had skin too dark

This is for the girls we gave up on
But could have saved, hurt by men
Who go on unpunished

Predators in the night
Also walk in the day

Don't forget, most rapes and attacks and murders

Are committed by the men close to you

Stranger danger
Family danger
Friend danger
Husband danger
Home becomes danger
Body is danger
Love is danger

True crime trailers auto-play when I open my browser,
Reminding me right before bedtime
With tight shots into the eyes of serial killers

Hollow voices I didn't ask to hear
Confessing their darkest sins to me,
Monotone and emotionless, like reading a grocery list
But then they'll crack a knowing smile
That haunts me through the night

And in my dreams, I'm always being hunted,
Clutching broken locks tight
Between my bleeding hands

Men color me purple
Passions shift to violence
Choking into *choking*
Until I know what it feels like
To be held underwater

It wouldn't surprise me to die at the hands of a man

Every date starts to taste like *Law and Order: SVU*
Sour adrenaline on my tongue
"Nice" feels like a tactic
"Charming" feels like *run!*
The perp gets away, there is no justice
Cut to black
Executive Producer Dick Wolf

Who can you be to me
Without at least three girls I trust
Vouching for you?

If you're going to kill me,
Just please, do it quickly

Even the "good" boys turn bad around their friends,
Condone coded language
As if it doesn't fuel the very system
In which we can't ever be safe

They've never understood how much
"Just words" have power,
How (even passive) participation feeds cycles of behavior
That start small but lead
To men holding down unwilling women,
To bodies buried in the woods,
Ripped clothes and blood and semen

Don't fucking tell me these things aren't connected
Don't make yourself out to be nonthreatening
If you won't stand up for us

It doesn't have to be this way just because it is
I've unlearned so much, but I guess y'all just aren't willing
You don't realize you make me feel unsafe in this world

I can feel it through all the women I've been before this,
Every woman I've ever met or will meet

Sure, Harvey Weinstein will rot in his jail cell
But is it still justice when it takes this long?
When the victims are the ones receiving death threats?
When Donald Tr*mp is still allowed to be president?

Men are shocked when I tell them
Without a beat of hesitation
I don't think I could ever fully love a son

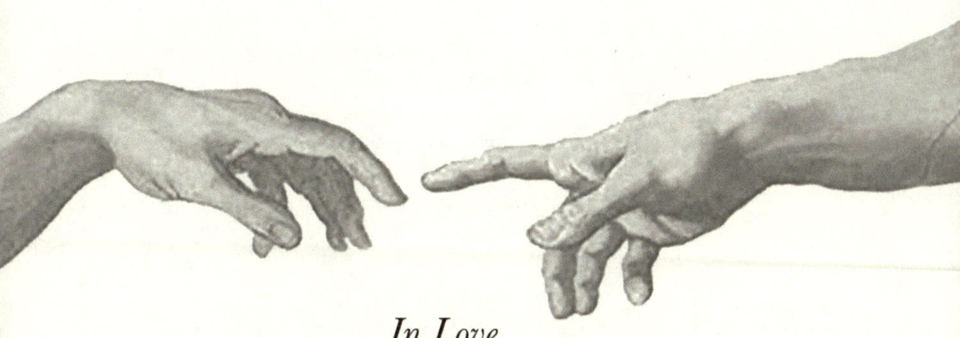

In Love,
at an Arm's Length

Early spring, with weddings and births and everything in handsome bloom
I try to be careful,
But nothing feels safe

Plan B gives me another kind of morning sickness
A foreign ache in my womb
Spreads out from the center,
Nausea seeps into the fingertips

How would you feel if I left you for a woman?

The moon is full and I'm ovulating,
We exchange longing looks
While Holly Miranda sings F*orever Young*

I smell like someone else's stress-smoken cigarettes
(You know I can't stand the smell anymore)

Who do you see when you look at me?
And would I even know her?

In bad dreams I'm kept in a case
Behind glass so clean you forget it's even there
My figure shiny and new,
Preserved forever twenty-five and turned on

You let me out when you feel like it,

A prize on your arm,
Your trophy wife

If this is happiness, you can take it back

I know you mean it sweet
But I don't want to be shown off

I'm more than pretty
More than soft
More than fuckable, functional, pliable, persuasive

More than memories to be immortalized
And forgotten
Like every word I leave behind

But I've stopped leaving words behind me
Can I no longer be a poet when I'm too in love?
That old fucking cliché—
Does it have to hurt for me to be inspired?

Hurt me good, break me back together
I don't want it to be true

I've got you where I didn't mean to want you
In love with me
But kept still at an arm's length
After all this time

I'm snuggled up beside you for half of the week
Taking in your love, trying not to take it
For granted

I play with words, your little brat
Press my skin against yours until you forget you're in love with me,
Demote me down to lust, just for the night

Can't I just be both the angel and the whore?
Leave out the shiny prize to show off in between?

I call you *daddy* in my head
You don't want to hear me say it
I'm so sorry

You hate when I talk about toxic masculinity
I'll bite my tongue harder
So you feel absolved

At my worst, eyes feel like hands
And I can't leave my body,
Can't wriggle out from the grip
Of a stare

At my worst, I leave the house
And drive in circles, back and forth
Between grocery stores and coffee shops,
Walking trails and pharmacies
That I can't go into
Because I can't stand to be beared witness to

At my worst I'm impatient
And needy and succinct,
No silver linings or rose-colored glasses
Left to find

At my worst I'm materialistic
And controlling and crazy,
Body buzzing with something foreign
I must get out of me

At my worst I see the worst in you—
The embedded-in good-old-boy image,
That little hint of boys-will-be-boys,
Red-blooded American
I'm too tired to try to teach you
To be better than good

I don't want to be your doll,
I'm soft and small and talk like a valley girl
But I know how to raise my voice,
To use my tongue like a dagger

I could bring a man to tears
But I leave it on the page instead

When you said you were proud of me
Oh, I could have wept

Until you clarified

When you said you were proud of me
You meant you were proud to have me

On your arm, in your bed
Are you proud of yourself?

It isn't like me to pick fights
My blood is still boiling

At my worst, my needs and desires
Are bottomless pits that can't be filled,
Gluttonous monsters you can only feed
And through me, oh, they beg

Say you'd die without me
Even though I know it isn't true
I don't know if anyone will ever love me this much
Again

Hold me until I can't be held anymore
I'm sorry but I need you to
Show me it would hurt to lose me

Like surgery without anesthesia
Be still my goddamn beating heart

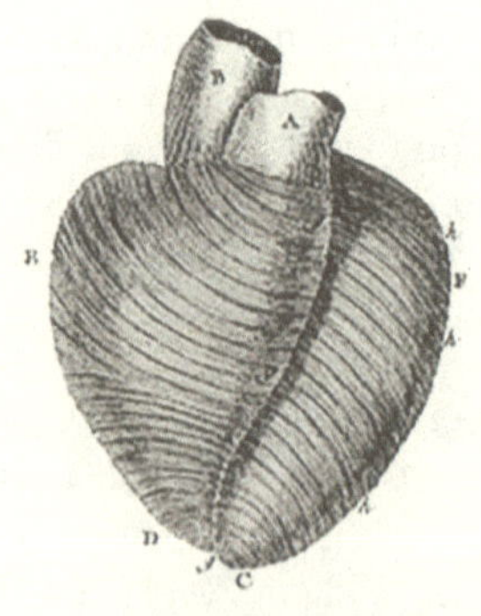

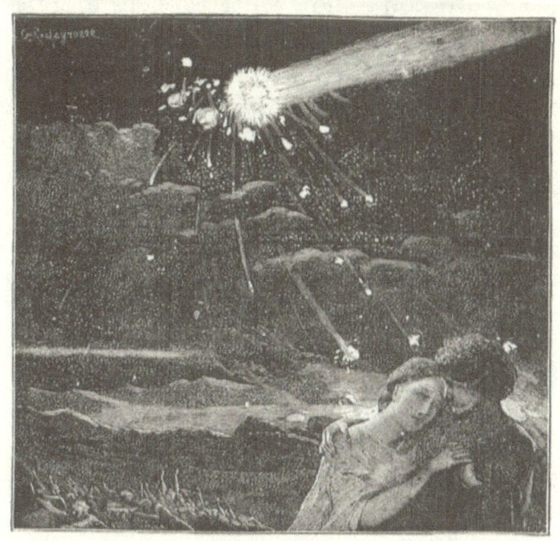

"STRANGERS TO THE UNIVERSAL PANIC."

the End of the World

I watch the skies set on fire, burning bright sirens across the world,
loud warnings on an astrological plane, ominous, to a biblical severity
Chaos rains down to the earth, singing her celestial music heard over the independent lights of vivid casinos in Oklahoma, surrounded by open road, and the deafening sound of the things we're not talking about, feelings of *forever* heightened by chronic threats of Armageddon
And trauma, left festering on the cutting room floor, covered up along with endemic violence and exploitation, until exposing well-known horrors of the rich and famous becomes the hot movement in

journalism, profound exposés written with a significant goal of generating clicks, surpassing the secondary purpose of change and progress in a largely violent society
Distress, engineering ad-revenue, while men mourn their fallen idols and blame naïve girls walking into evil traps, as if they thought they had a choice, as if we don't know what happens to girls who say *no*, sickening humanness aggressively concealed beneath legend, money and power, admiration and under-the-table promises made between differing levels of platform and influence, trading breadcrumbs of clout for devoted confidentiality in hotel rooms and in the daylight
Shedding a sobering glow on the ordinary people protecting monsters, terrified of becoming divorced from celebrity, therefore offering half-assed, transparent apologies, all hoping they won't have to be held accountable for repulsive actions once swept under the rug by active enablers to abuse of power, and for what? They ask hollow atonement for actions they'd joyously continue if promised eternal discretion—what they thought of as birthright within
The boys clubs, and the many women benefiting from their influence, complicit participants publicly condemning the vulgar behaviors in which they've participated through excusing, overlooking, tolerating, and contributing to vile spaces in time, sufferings that sometimes anchor young lives, trapped in the same place for years
While we worship actors and their performative activism, wearing black on red carpets while still supporting Roman Polanski and letting men they call friends and brothers continue to question the credibility of traumatized women, both for yelling too loudly and for taking too long to speak up, anger or silence, both somehow suspect in the eyes of the public
And no amount of evidence will ever force them to stop separating artist from the art, dancing in the club to the voices of rapists

Ancient rulers are reborn into an evolved state of evil, salivating for
another shot at apocalyptic power over mankind and land,
women and their bodies, these prevalent cult-leaders existing
in the mainstream, recruiting through popular airwaves
condemned and mocked by gentler souls who underestimate
the predominance of malicious energy in our tumultuous
times

Plagues present themselves, unsupervised, one at a time,
and then all at once—constant warnings of the end
of our world as we know it

While we're taking our pills to offset the nerves, and the
pills to offset the symptoms of the pills to offset the
nerves

We fall asleep watching shows that give us a glimpse into
nauseating luxury, an inexcusable excess thrown in
the faces of hungry hardworking people begging on
the streets for spare change, met with disgust by
luckier, less-deserving people who blame the
disenfranchised for the evil results of capitalism,

People who donate to shady charities for a fucking tax
break and a sense of superior satisfaction, who look
at good people cast to the streets as subhuman

Who worship capitalism in the name of God and country
and The American Dream

As if capitalism seeks to empower anyone outside of the
historically empowered, hoarding billions made on
the underpaid labor of the diligent, the starving, the
dying

Do you love beauty?

Or do you cling to her?

A form of Stockholm syndrome passed down through
generations of women who confuse the oppression
of beauty ideals with empowerment—a
heartbreaking relationship with a beautiful,
terrifying industry whose greatest fear is for you to
transcend the tedious ideals of perfection and
completion, to understand

The importance of engraining in ourselves a disgust at
the first signs of misogyny—so deep that we pass it
down to our daughters and theirs, evolving past the
point of tolerating having our personhood
determined by violent beings who do not value us
as people

We can not entertain the men who speak of chaos as the eighth wonder of the world, who amuse the idea of genocide, rebranding itself as noble patriotism, who carry racism and misogyny in the name of tradition, white terrorism safeguarded by free-speech, allowed easily to mobilize, crossing over lines like they're gateways to heaven, and
Finding welcome solace in those who confuse sexual impulse with assault and pedophilia, applauding predators for "seeking help"—all smoke and mirrors in a desperate attempt to change the narrative of reality
Do not mourn the inconvenienced lives of corrupt, perverted legends—idols, torn down from Hollywood, or Silicon Valley, or whatever glorified standing on earth,
The dead perpetrators expelled from heaven, and everywhere in between heaven and eternal damnation
These demons walk among us
It is not our burden to find it in us to forgive
I say—let them burn

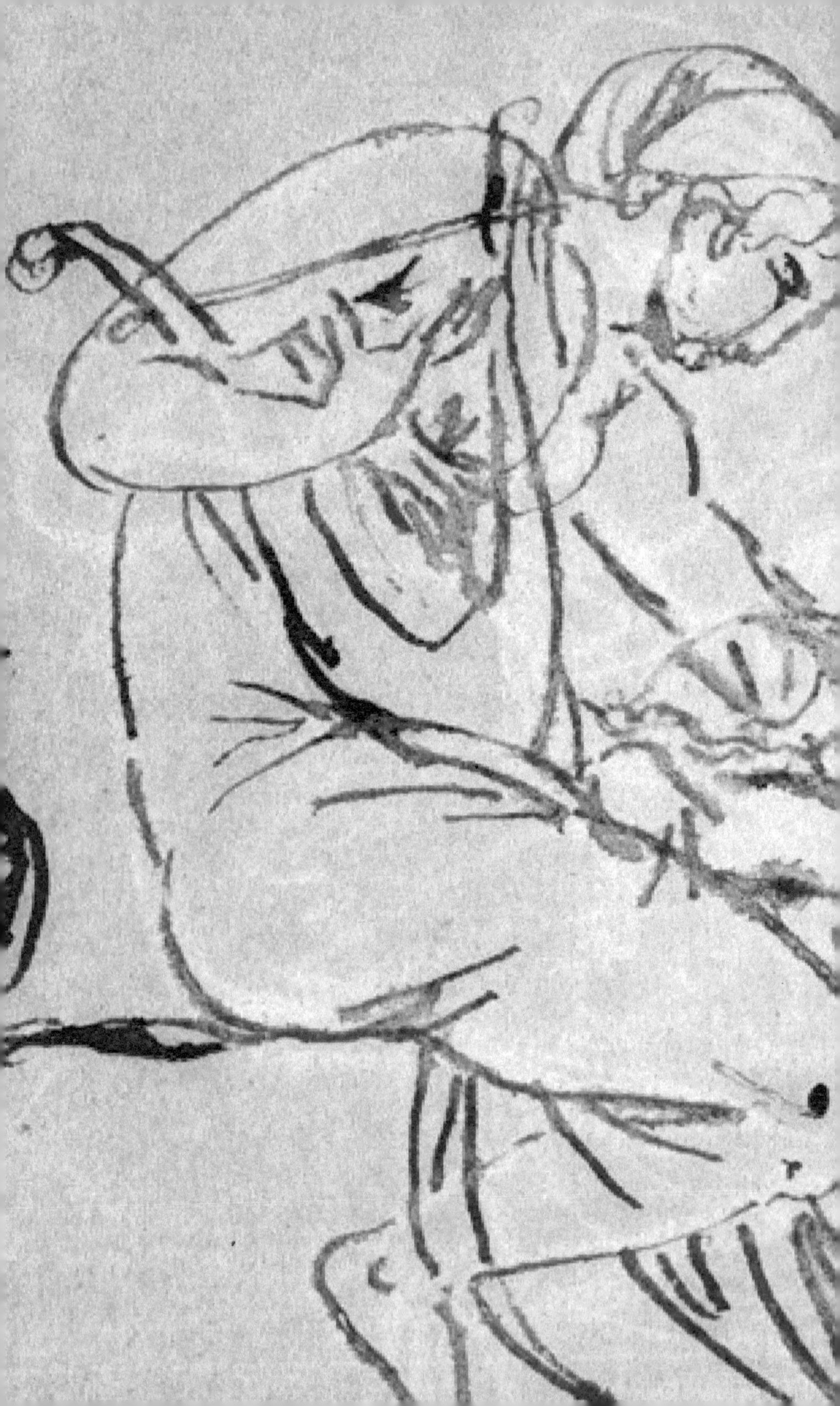

ACT II

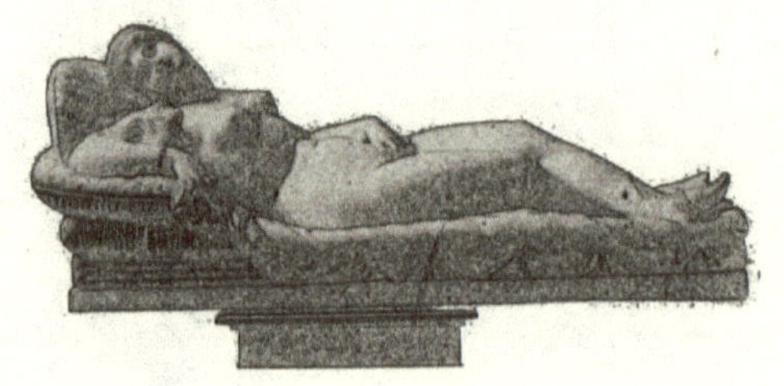

Fruit Flies

My dream is dead, and there's a candlelight vigil just for the two of us
Because we can't tell

The flies all died, I think they knew before we did
That nothing is permanent

Grieving is our secret, we wear black and leather
And turn the shop into our own disco bar between transactions

Do we cover the walls in beauty, or start tearing them down?

We smile while secretly searching on Google for *how to PR your heartbreak,*
Everything is not okay!

Fixed signs, forced into flux
While we sweat out the summer heat

Sit in the window while you can babe,
This is going to hurt like hell

I decorate my bedroom with every flower that ever died here,
We're the only two blooms left alive

I bathe in soft yellow peony petals
Maybe if I soak in them long enough, I'll wake up

I watch the cop outside rest his hand on his gun
I've never felt less protected

A stranger tells me *it's cute,*
But it doesn't look like enough to keep the lights on

Others pitch us products—shampoo and art and flowers and face masks
No one knows that they pour pink Himalayan salt in our wounds

the Blush on my Cheeks Felt Brighter a Year Ago

It's sticky outside
A man on the sidewalk stares at me as I walk by,
His hand in his pants

I learned at age 12
My body will always be sexualized
Whether I want it or not

So why not learn to want it?

The blush on my cheeks
Felt brighter a year ago

My body is beautiful
My body is ugly
Both home and foreign
Controversial and conventional

Taboo and universal
Everyone's and no one's
Some incoherent days, not even mine

But I'm here, so why not look?

I'm too old to be this young and stupid
Dancing in the club to this sad shit,
Wretched poems disguised as pop songs in September

But I can't stop hitting repeat

It's true—
No one comes along for the ride to rock bottom

I'm worse for wear
This is what they meant by *for better or for worse*?

I know we never exchanged vows
Are you still willing to stay by my side?

This is the aftermath of the morning's soft rain,
A taste of autumn
I can't spit back out

I see my psychologist on Friday the 13th
Good thing I was never superstitious
Black cats never brought luck worse than life came with
Find a penny, pick it up...
Makes no difference to me

I learn to survive, to read body language,
To recognize when a man clenches in anger
To know people include too many details
When they're lying

I lean into my writing,
Any attempt to offset
Depression amnesia

But the poet chooses a solitary art, her hands
Resting on the home keys,
An abstract threat in her partner's mind
(Please don't hold it against me)

Is there power in writing about the people who've hurt us?
Or does that give *them* the power?
Of relevance, of proven thought
In the writer's mind?

Do we really heal through this documentation?
Through being seen and heard in words sublime?

If poetry is archaic, then what the fuck
Do you think you're singing along to?

At night, in the car,
When belting feels the closest you can get to finding yourself?

Words—not only their meanings, their weight,
Their baggage, their order
But their physical sound, the way they look written,

The shapes they form
And the texture in your mouth

We rename ourselves in letters and sounds that fit better
Hem and shorten the arms, tailor in the waist
Until it feels right
I want my name to taste sweet

Put me back on repeat and
Wave goodbye to my misplaced ambitions
I know I'm not as replaceable as you think I am

I can't keep crying wolf
And forgetting to take my meds

But my dream is dead
Is dead is dead
And now I can't sleep

WLW
Who Sometimes (Maybe?) Loves Men

let me never be the girl
who goes home to a man
and tucks her gayness away
for safekeeping

like a necklace to unclasp
and rip from my neck, shut in a drawer
next to the bed

like something to hide
from the fainter of heart,
not to be mentioned over dinner

like something unpleasant
and best not to be spoken of
in *his* company

like something possible
to remove from myself,
to pluck away gently
without spilling blood,
without last dying, queer-little breath

my love is gracious and complex
but with a man, becomes withholding
and dissatisfied and resentful
of my feeling like
a kept woman

I can't deny my panic
in a man pulling my hand toward his crotch,
a feeling of violence I can't quite put into words

but I love him I tell myself
he would never hurt me
so why does this hurt?

I swallow my pride, try not to wear the guilt
too boldly, and fight with myself
before I say yes or no,
only to lose
either way

I rarely think of ex boyfriends
but I still dream about the girl who kissed me that one night
and texted the next morning
to say how glad she was to have met me
and so lovingly called me a dyke
like it was the most beautiful word ever written

my love feels its purest when it's gay—
soft face falling asleep on my right tit gay
crying together at her apartment on the first date gay
shared experience that doesn't need explaining gay
clingy touchy-feely intoxicating gay
power play without the actual imbalance of power gay
another body I'm not afraid to touch gay
woman kissing woman without an audience gay
tongue to cunt, come so hard you cry fucking gay

I've unlearned the tolerance
to let any man
(or biphobic woman
or anyone else)
act as the gatekeeper
of my identity

queer and sapphic,
but unsure
of how far into heteronormativity
my love can reach

make no mistake—
my queerness is still with me
when I try to love a man

in my every gay-ass little touch
in my every overbearing kiss
in the way that I fuck
and tease and long

in the depths of my heart
and at the core of my being

you'd better know
you're being loved
by a gay girl

Offerings for Aphrodite

What's left beneath, when the city lights go out and we're all alone in the world we've created, devoid of community?

In delirious congregation, do you pray for me? When you're making a scene, singing songs about Venus, risen up from the sea to save us from the things we hate inside ourselves?
Can we strip away at our shallowest anxieties, as a collective offering for Aphrodite—imperfections of the flesh, insidious little uncertainties we've projected all around us, trying to run from what was never there, never significant?
I want the sky wrapped around me, even still, surrounded by terrifying angels, too good for humanity—for what we've made of it, with such unclear intentions.

What love is left in our world?

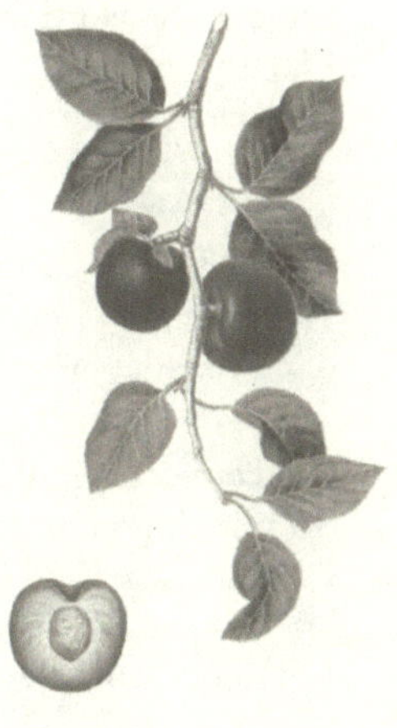

I Wrote a Poem While You Talked in Your Sleep

Awake in the night, riddled with unbearable cramps,
Your arm rested on my waist, heavy with your sleep,
I write this in Notes on my dimly lit phone

You sleep-talk about public records; violently awake,
I dream of cutting open my abdomen
And tearing out the thing some Republicans think
Makes me a woman

I swell with my own fertility, amazed and horrified
I want to give this motherly piece of me away,
Offer up my womb to someone more deserving

I want to hold you so tight I swallow you into me
Consumed with lover, never with child
At times, I feel so wholly woman
Others, the word feels too big for me, ill-fitting
Like the clothes I'm still hoarding after years
Of collecting dust
(I am my mother's daughter)

It's 3:33 in the morning, your bedroom pitch black
With the heavy curtains you put up
That one day when my head hurt

I'm kept company by the sound of artificial rain I play
So I don't go crazy with the quiet—
I can feel the hum faintly in my thumb as I type this

I'm angry from the pain, angry *at* the pain,

Angry at my body for making me feel this, angry at you,
For no reason

I'm awake long enough my eyes adjust to the dark
And start creating moving shapes I try not to follow
In the mirror

You feel me tossing, tell me to wake you if I need anything
But you're quietly snoring before you finish your sentence

I try to keep my crying as small and soft as possible
So drunk on poems I almost tell you I'm in love with you

I still remind myself not to throw up meals
I scratch my skin when I go without sleep
I dance in Polaroid flashes
I never get around to mailing thank you notes
You know who I am

In the summers, I am so much flesh—
All rubbing thighs and big pink areolas bouncing asexually
With my each heavy step

The city shakes under my weight
Businessmen stick to the sour sweat on my forehead

I put out a book
Share too much of myself
Post my nipples online to feel seen
Grow out a strip of pubic hair for the first time in my life
(I'm a fucking adult!)
Redact poems before giving them to my mother
Have sex with a forty-two-year-old
Graduate therapy

But I can't cook for myself,
Can't convince myself to nourish

My house isn't homey
And the garbage disposal hasn't worked in five years

Left alone in your apartment
With the key you gave me last week

Through no fault of yours, I feel like you're testing me

I send you voice recordings of me
Lounged cozily in your condo,
Wrapped up in the blanket you keep strewn
Over the couch,
Reciting poetry by Maggie Nelson into my phone

This one is five minutes long, and every time I stumble
Over my words, I erase and begin again, from the top,
Always trying to sound like it's the first time—
Casual, soft, uncalculated

I've forgotten your living room walls are covered
In your hunt—so many birds, forever preserved
In mid-flight

I try not to guess how many guns you have hidden
I know you
I love you
I repress parts of you
Who are you?

Golden Spiral

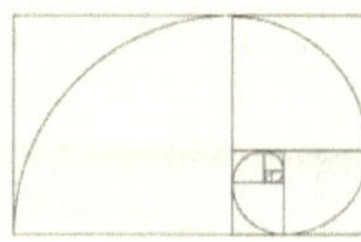

I'm pausing to look back,
to notice and acknowledge the patterns I've fallen into
and tripped over every time

I was never trusting,
but was still too trusting

calm, raspy voices
whisper melodic proclamations
of hopeless devotion and undying love,
tainted by the constant, abstract threat
of so many ways of leaving

how many times did I have to vocalize
my fear of abandonment?
so deep, so disturbing, so defining

and finally, validated
by the culmination of all that we put into this—
remnants of a person
who showed me the versions of themself
they thought I was capable of loving,
instead of something genuine and whole, instead of truth

my noble fucking darling, were you really "protecting me"
by insulting my capacity for offering,
for the darknesses I could stomach?

even after I fell open for you,
deep-throated the holiest of lies,
and recklessly ignored
your flashing-red signs of manipulation

using me for extra dopamine
for affection
for body
for tits and cunt
for sweet small voice
that never talked back

for my loving you
the only way I've ever known how—

blind and generous
to the point of ruin

I'm so goddamn tired
of rebuilding men who pretend
to be weak and wounded,
something to nurture
until the roses start to wilt
and true colors run wild

and you told me I should be so lucky,
so fucking grateful for your partial love
for your half attention
for your crumbs of respect
when you could tell I was at my breaking point,
so much hopeless devotion
for two days after I'd speak my mind

and then you'd forget you'd promised to try,
that you meant it for real, this time

is this what I'd deluded myself into thinking?
that as long as you weren't hurting me physically,
then this was love?

let me spiral out of control
as long as I'm spiraling in a Fibonacci sequence,
perfect and mesmerizing
and endless

you'd leave voicemails
arguing in favor of forgiveness,
playing to all of my most merciful tendencies, asking

can we be brought back?

each syllable you spoke
was another pin prick

this is what I meant, writing about ghosts
so far in the past I shouldn't remember
the little things, the small expressions, the freckle
in your eye

but on the darkest of days, I still love you to pieces
not you, but the you you could've been
without the games and the secrets
without the deep, dark double life

Capitalism is Evil.
Trust No One.

Winter days fall shorter but feel just as long
The American Dream was always just a dream,
Propaganda from the men at the top
Get out while you can, oh but you can never get out

Welcome to your life,
The goddamn grind
Is never-ending

We become machines:
Clock in
Clock out
Carve corporate policies into our flesh
Go home and undress
Branded by work

Try to sleep at night without dreaming
Of unanswered emails and budget spreadsheets,
Angry men with expensive suits
And salaries that could feed entire cities

Of thousand-pound palettes needing to be unboxed,
Of the bottom line
And the layoffs,
Health insurance
And how many days until payday

Your at work friends aren't your friends
Your friends are taking notes

They'll say they care
But can't be bothered to spell your name right,
Twist your words so far they take a shape
That no longer fits in your mouth

Don't bite the hand that claims to feed you,
Oh it'll feed you just enough that you can't quite starve
Your sanity impaled on sharp teeth
Didn't they tell you? It's your job to sharpen them

Don't complain about unfair pay and policies
Or they'll send you to a psychiatrist
And say being gaslit is a pre-existing condition

Being told you're emotionally unstable hits harder
When you thought you had a friend in the room

That HR lady really said I was paranoid!
No one's losing their job
But jokes on her, she got laid off a few days later
It isn't funny, but what can you do other than laugh?

No one's losing their job
But when someone finally quits
It's apparently "not in the budget" to replace them
So what's the truth?

Give them years of your life and they'll repay you
By pushing you down just to get to the top,
Claim your work as their own,
They'll never let you get ahead

Capitalism is watching you on the security cameras
Give him your blood sweat and tears
But, for fuck's sake, look professional!

The generational wealth gap
The gender wealth gap
The racial wealth gap
The gaps in my memory

Absent management
Micromanagement
Nowhere to be found,

But also looking over my shoulder,
My powdery blush on the bottom of your shoes
From climbing over me

I asked to grow
They pulled out profit and loss statements
Cut me off at the root
Won't allow me to be watered

Twice minimum wage still isn't enough to live on
Capitalism wants us controlled,
Dead inside but not quite dead, because dead kids
Can't do labor

They'll call you lazy but don't allow overtime
Well, legally we only have to give you 30 hours a week

If this doesn't work for you, you're free to go
We're not holding you hostage
From the mouth of a girl whose hair I once stroked
With her head in my lap at two in the morning

After holding her hand while ink went into her skin,
After buying me drinks at that mescal bar,
After crying together
And begging me to stay the night

From the mouth of a girl
Who doesn't care if I starve,
So much can change in a year

I asked for crumbs,
Got my stomach pumped instead

I've got to get out of this company before my book is done
Or I'm for sure getting fired for this

To be fired for a poem—
Oh, what a way to go

To break the very strings
With which you strung me along

Velvet Hotel Rooms

I still think about those late nights at karaoke
singing Dolly Parton and Patsy Cline,
Nina Simone and *Some Velvet Morning,*
dancing below the neon lights and disco balls
by the side of the road

she looks so stunning in the stupid dive-bar spotlights,
reciting her own made-up lyrics
to the tune of my favorite love songs
when she's three drinks deep and she starts to feel
uninhibited

she pulls me toward her with a touch I know is innocuous,
the only display of synchronized desire and protection
I've felt in years, a safe home I just want to settle into

but every time feels like it's the last,
fleeting, by our own design, leaving us wondering why
we're both so terrified of anything with permanence
but so boldly vulnerable,
like open books with pages torn out, shredded and buried
so deep they may never be recovered,
lost to the passage of time

made translucent
from the beginning, but implanted still
somewhere within so many congested memories
of back when

but she didn't know me then

I feed her reassurance—the only thing I know how to offer
she feeds me ice-cold whiskey to numb the sting
of my unrepressed memories, doting on me,
her passive, temporary partner

kissing in our secret space here
with rococo paintings of angels looking past
the visual manifestations of our pain
marked for reminiscing in the moments
of madness I don't want anymore

she's the only one who can tell
when I need her to stop touching me
and who does so without uncertainty, without judgment,
without resentment held against me in silence,
bottled up until it's too late to come back from

I Want to Cry by a Body of Water

I want to cry by a body of water
Adding a piece of myself to the current
Leaving, but always coming back

I want for the waves to lap at my legs
Hitting me with the sound of the quiet sea
Some small form of baptism

I want to sob in a soaking wet, satin slip dress
Let it cling to my body
Without letting go

I want to float, to feel weightless and
Drift away from the ground as an exercise in patience,
To learn to trust in things
Outside of myself

I want to be a small fleck of light on water,
A glimmering dance moving with the planet

When the sun sets, I want to wash back to shore,
To feel the twilight greet me,
The sky a shade of lilac
I want to put my mouth on—

To suckle on the atmosphere,
To be nourished by the wind

I want to wear fuchsia in a canopy of kelly green
Saturated opposites, each heightening the other

I want to walk barefoot in the dirt and the grass
Feeling each small texture beneath my every step

I want to feel the earth in the early morning
When no one else does, alone with the elements,
Trying to understand them,
And seeing if they understand me

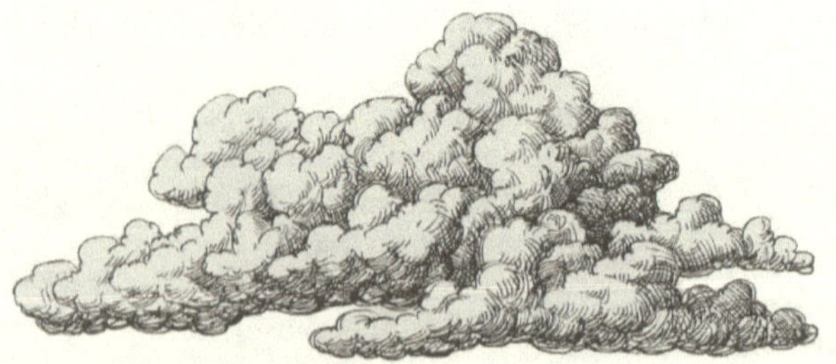

It Feels Good Until It Doesn't

It's Wednesday night and I'm making a conscious decision:
we're trying life one more time

I get writer's block when my shop closes down
I'm a career-orphan for the second time in six months,
passed from home to home,
hoping someone will want to keep me
(I'm that little puppy your mother says you can't have, another little mouth to feed just isn't in the budget)

I have migraines every day and hurt myself twice a week,
I have sex I don't want, abstain from solid foods,
and recreate bruises from past accidents so the marks don't feel like mine

Someone tells me they look like galaxies;
in the heat of the summer, I can only hide so much

My bosses sit me down and ask me not to kill myself
Everyone is afraid; I can't look you in the eye
and tell you not to be

I'm afraid, too

I never had a hard exterior, you just thought I did
The bathrooms here are perfect for crying,
less perfect for liking your reflection in the mirror

I exist all day in harsh overhead lighting
that doesn't flatter any us
and hurts my eyes and head by noon

Sometimes voices murmur in the distance
The sound carries in, the vessels don't

I fall in love for five minutes with every curly-haired, gay-adjacent
girl who smiles at me,
every maybe-dyke I pass on the sidewalk,
every someone who could potentially understand me

I hiss with the desert scents I've slathered onto my skin,
slipping in and out of outfits
until I feel okay enough to exist,
shifting my shapes between feminine and boxy, slip dresses and
shoulder-padded blazers
but nothing fits

I'm so tired of being a body
but my instincts tell me
lean the fuck in;
if you have to be a body, be a body

I let myself fall addicted to touch,
to being admired
I sleep with couples when I need more attention
than one person can give me
It feels good until it doesn't

Sunlight whispers on my bare chest,
growing louder as she rises
until she's shaking me awake
like a mother who's lost her patience
but I don't mean to be stubborn, I just don't know how to get out of
bed this week

I fight the urge to scream at people who don't deserve it
just so someone will have to hear me

Who the fuck do I think I am?
You sad sack, you dumb little girl who knows better
than to create points of contention
out of nothing

I spend my shifts with the space heater
while the books curl and warp from the cold
All of us are falling apart

I sit still, write bad poems like this one and get paid
It isn't fair of me to complain

The bubbly pop music tries to lift my mood
I spiral to the beat of it,
let my laptop battery run down to 3 percent
(living on the edge)

Do they have a pill that makes you feel fulfilled?

I should know by now that I feel this every summer—
trapped and tethered to a stagnant life
with nothing more than this to offer me

Every summer, it's true

Tenderness

I.
How divine it will be
if we're still together when the air gets cold,
to be held with the windows open,
the smell of outside
crawling into your bed with us

II.
Heavy thunder claps while we fuck,
nature's warm company illuminating our skin,
rain drowned out by fervent breaths
gasping for longer nights

III.
I jolt awake at four a.m., moan softly
in pain from my bad dreams
until you scoop me up in your big arms and whisper
I've got you, baby

This is tenderness

IV.
Cry with me, darling,
please cry with me

V.
Do you know you could rip my heart out?
Love is always porous,
dripping out faster than it can collect
in me

VI.

All-consuming,
lovely and terrifying,
spit in my mouth
to keep me from saying too much

VII.

To be in control of being controlled—
slapped around when I want to be,
demeaned, but I know you don't mean it
held down and tight, fucked and swaddled,
baby and whore, bitch and sweet angel

VIII.

There is gentleness in
leaving marks

Like holding a cry tight inside your throat,
like a small incision to relieve pressure,
like coming while making eye contact

IX.

Take and withhold,
restrict and deny
me until you're ready to give in

X.

I leave behind these words
for when you can't sleep at night
and the dark air tastes like danger
or longing or uncertainty
or your lover's wet hair

For when you can't sleep at night
and the moonlight laughs in your face,
sheds a glow on the empty space beside you

For when you fall in love again
and never say my name aloud...
I leave behind these words

XI.

But what shape was I ever in your hands?
Soil and salt water bending to fill any container,
to wrap dedicatedly around any lover,
to take and envelop, flesh and liquid,
warm breath and cunt

XII.

It's not true what they say, you know—
the first cut is never the deepest
and it hurts just as bad
the second time around

XIII.

Lick my broken heart clean of your love,
tasting each rough wound
so that we both remember

I don't want to be forgotten

Visions of Eden

where holy lights shine through tethered skies,
angelic prisms reflect on imaginary barriers—
the transparent gates to keep evil out,
or beauty in, preserved
or held hostage, begging to break free
and driven to a point of madness

bleeding under fingernails from trying to claw a way out
of what everyone thinks they want,
kept in like caged zoo animals, living
only as a form of entertainment
for the masses to tap on glass and awake from short naps—
one of so few escapes from this illusion of reality

predatory eyes grope at the curves of heaven
clinging on to the legend, the myth of purity
until they know she's been tampered with,
evolving to fit within
false windows into paradise

we're trying to erase what heaven forgets, but every other dwelling
remembers

A Cry in Malibu

I hide a nosebleed in the sky
And try not to throw up my nausea meds.

I can still picture the orange-flavored sick
Of my childhood road trips,
Picky snacks regurgitated
On the shoulder of the highway.

I take small sips of cold water,
Chew ice to feel grounded,
Take deep breaths and let them out slowly.

Our bodies work against us.
They took my mother's uterus
When she was bleeding to death
With fertility.

Everyone at LAX is in love,
Reunited with tight embraces,
Kissing like they've been separated by war.

I want to cry, but California won't let me.
(Maybe it's impossible to cry in purgatory)

My friend says
You can have a cry in Malibu
But the beauty of the ocean dries me up,
My attention grabbed by vibrant pastels
Until I can't feel anything.

The bright blue waters breathe in and out with me,
Mirror what I feel inside, calm and fluid.

This is pure contentment
Is without a care
Is being bodiless
Is being free.

I fall asleep in the sun,
Soak up vitamin D
For what feels like the first time,
Come home pinker
And with more spots to stress about
Back in the harsh light of Texas.

Flying over the ocean,
I sit awake, realizing how easily
It could swallow me.

Pinned against the man next to me
Taking up parts of my space,
Everything is vast and crammed,
Endless
And claustrophobic.

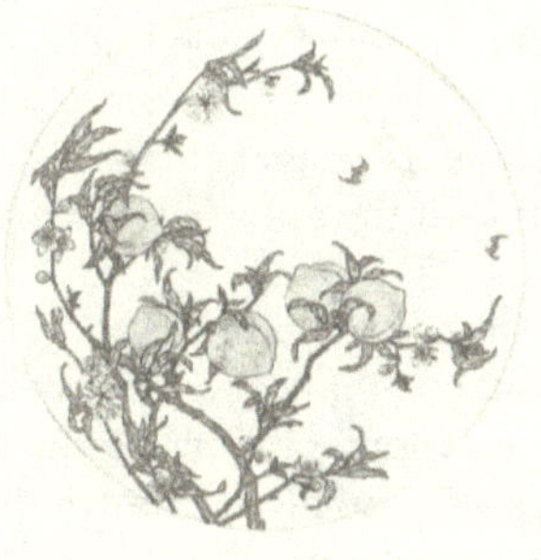

Sea Foam

I was born from the waves on the West Coast shoreline, wading in soft
green waters, clutching at the sands, learning to walk all over again
I succumb to new pressures, sprout limbs, organs, and fuzz, surrender
my lungs, practice breathing until the mechanics of it start to make
sense to me
My body is a machine working on overdrive, trying not to forget to
keep my heart beating at all times
How can I focus on anything but survival?

My hair grows longer, smells of sea salt, and falls out in micro-
amounts—strands and tresses of me left behind for ghosts and lovers
to remember me by
I learn the importance of language, of evanescence, of will
I learn of temptation; I eat the apple every time

Living becomes almost second nature
I breathe in air without coughing and pay my bills on time
Still, I am mostly water, forever influenced by the changing tides, my
moods and consciousness ebbing and flowing with the early August
morning Venice Beach sea foam

I listen to ocean sounds when I sleep, reminding me of home,
And dream of the texture of algae, of slow-dancing green, of my mother
I bathe in Lake Michigan; I lay in bathtubs with my clothes on

Angelic statues at museums spark memories of familiar bodies
My menstrual cycle syncs up with every body of water
We move together, breathe together, bleed together
And meet for book club on Wednesday on the ocean floor
We read *the Argonauts* underwater; an octopus giggles

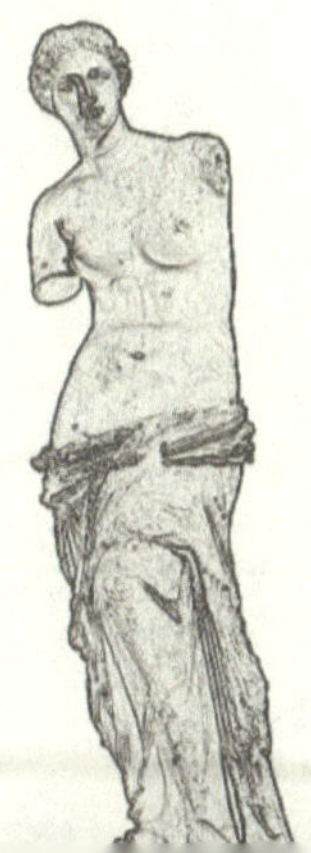

INTERMISSION:

Selected images depicting the energy of Venus

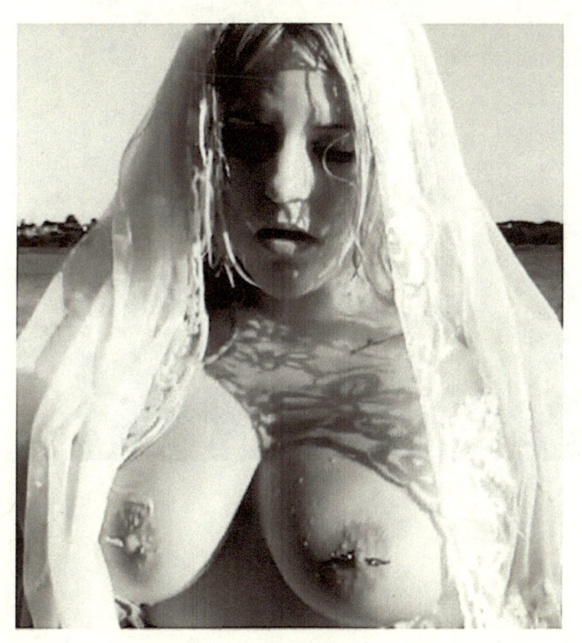

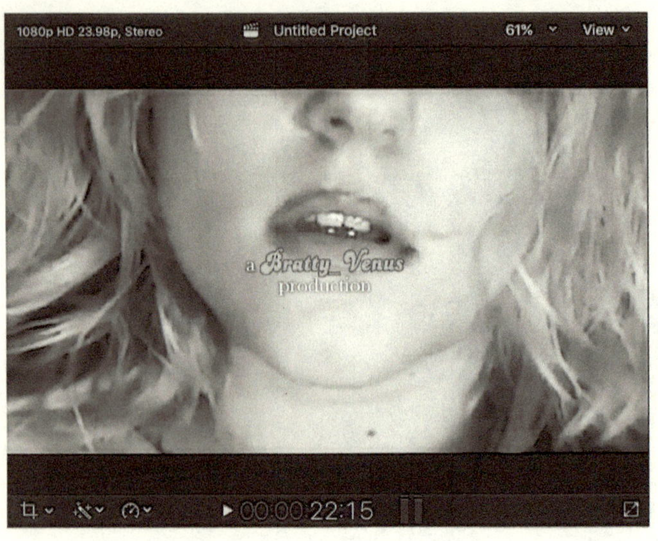

THIS PROJECT IS UNAPOLOGETICALLY AND EXPLICITLY ABOUT MY OWN PLEASURE, AND ANY PLEASURE YOU MAY EXPERIENCE AS THE VIEWER IS BEING GRANTED TO YOU, BY ME, ON MY OWN TERMS, THROUGH MY OWN GAZE.

xx Venus

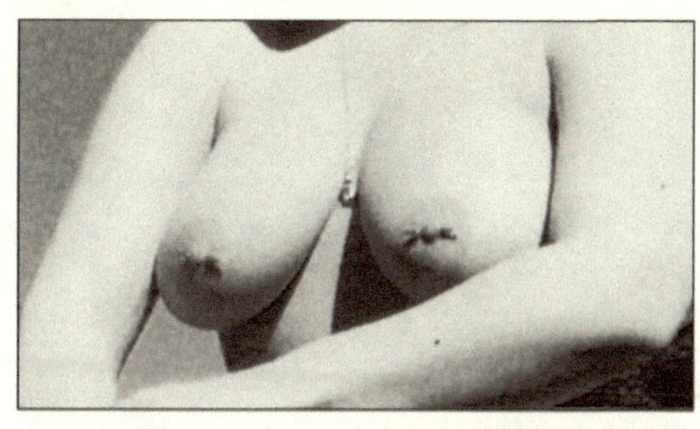

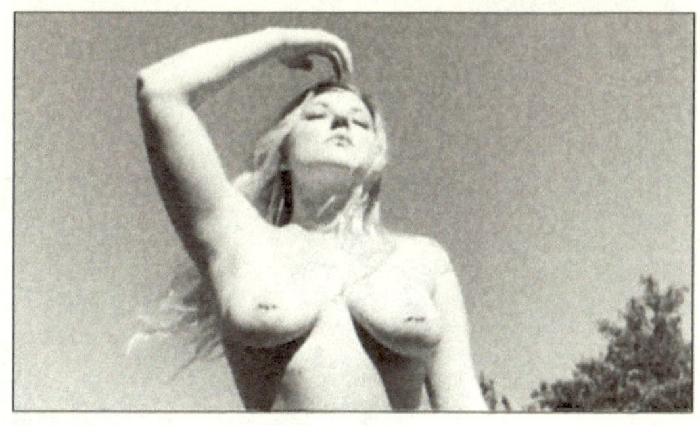

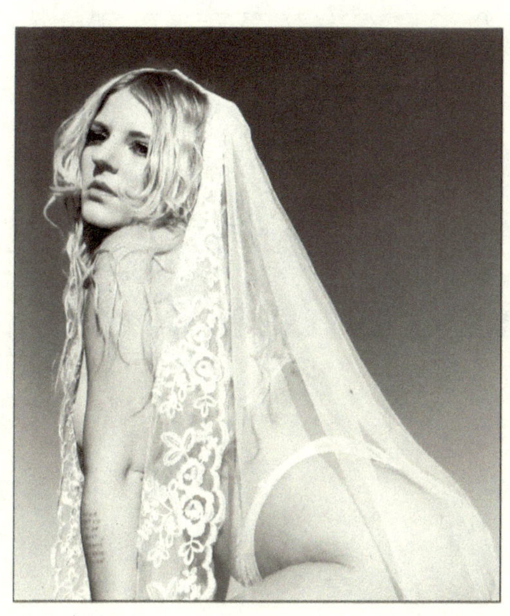

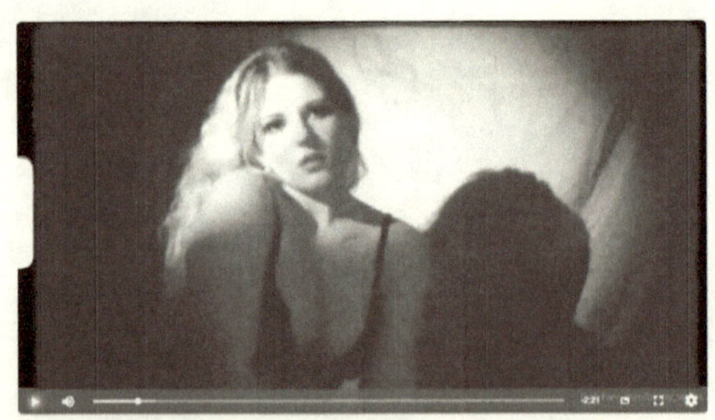

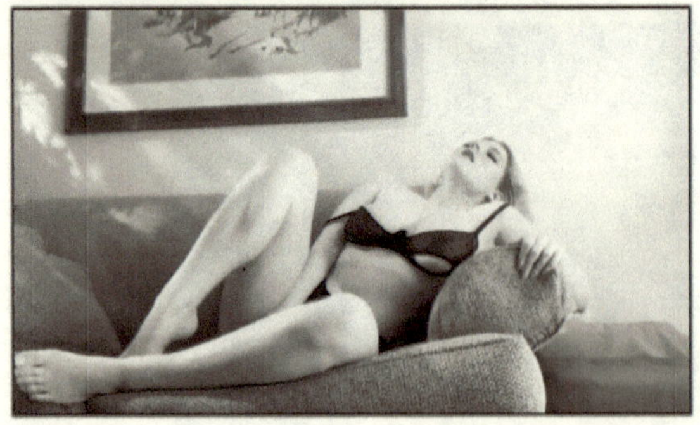

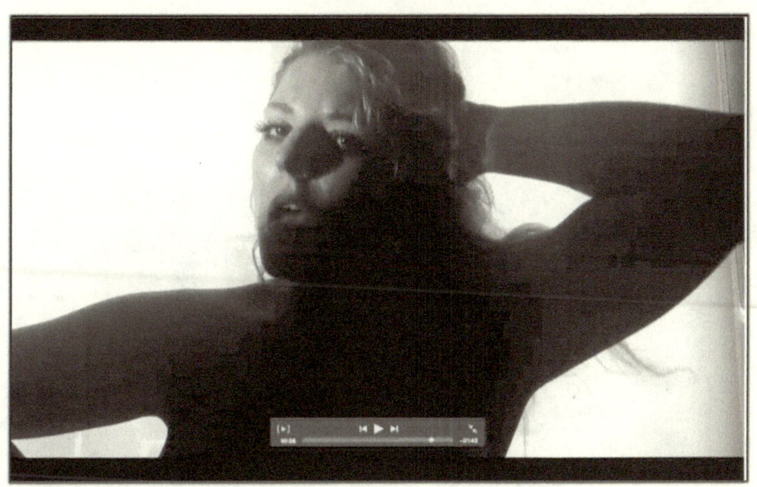

BUT ONE THING
FEELS CERTAIN-

IN EVERY LIFE,
IN EVERY BODY,
I'VE FOUND MY
OWN WAY
OF BEING A WHORE.

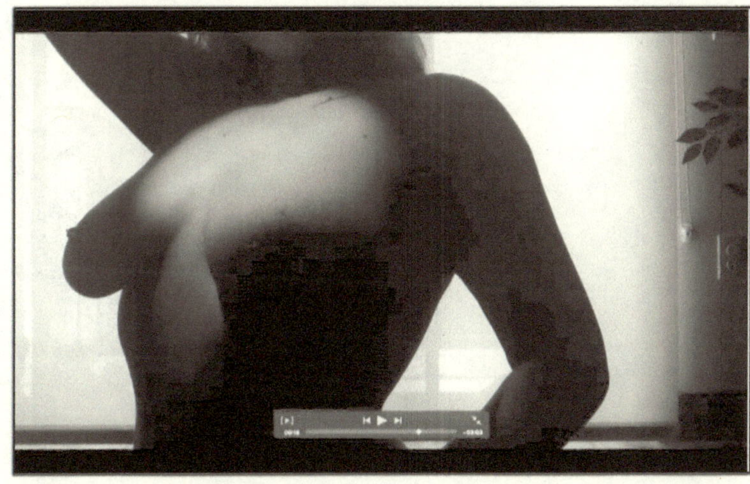

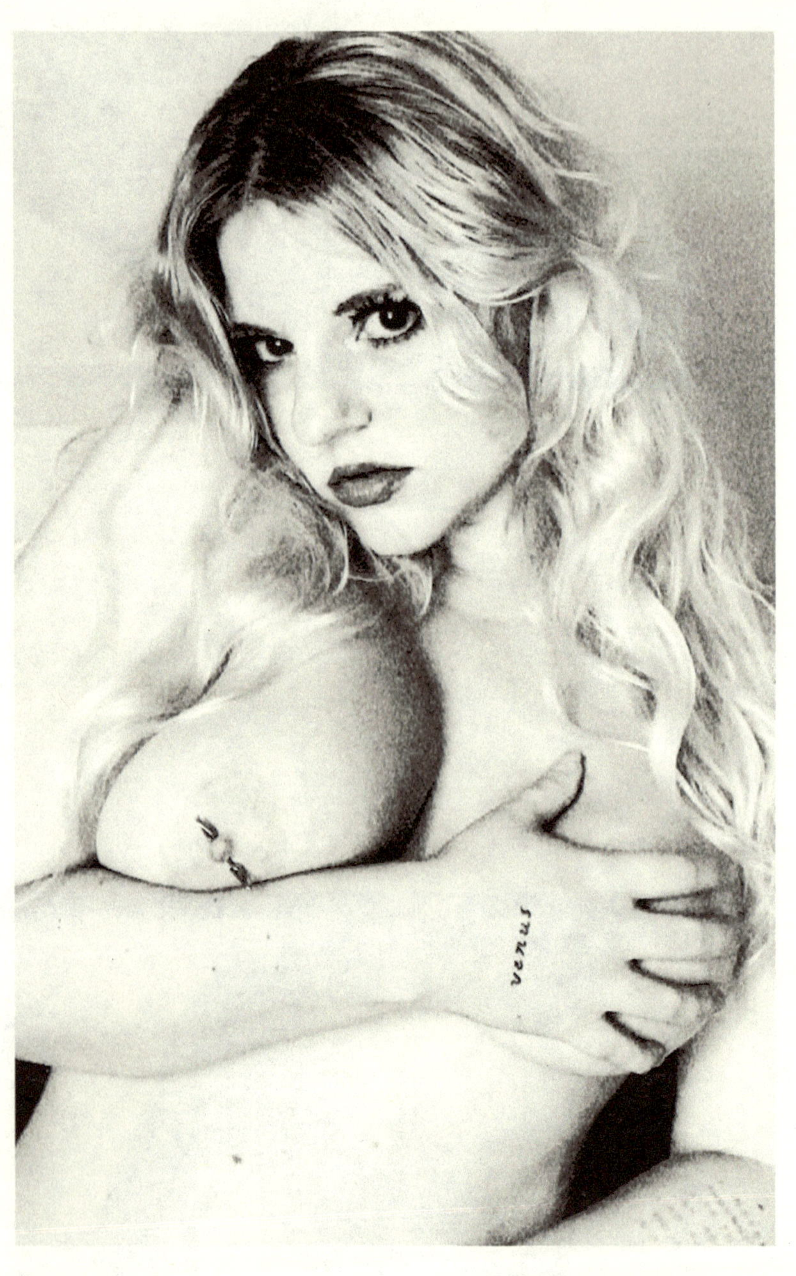
venus

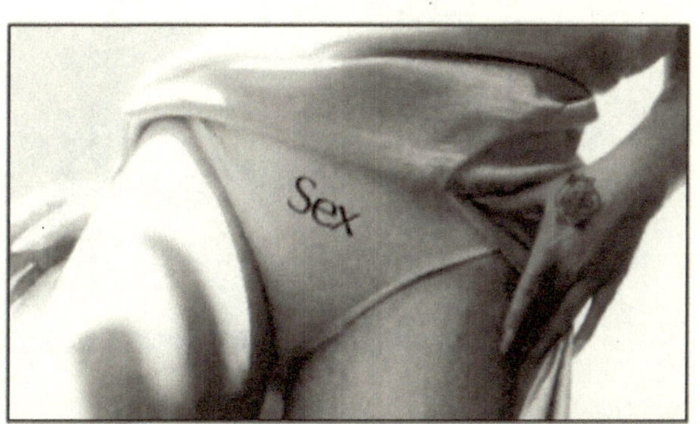
Sex

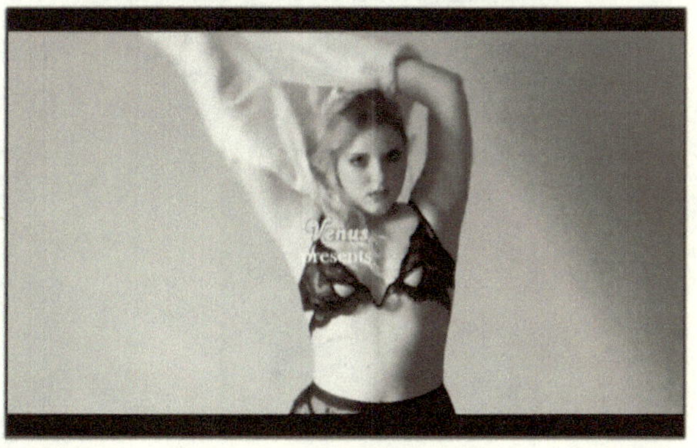
Venus
presents

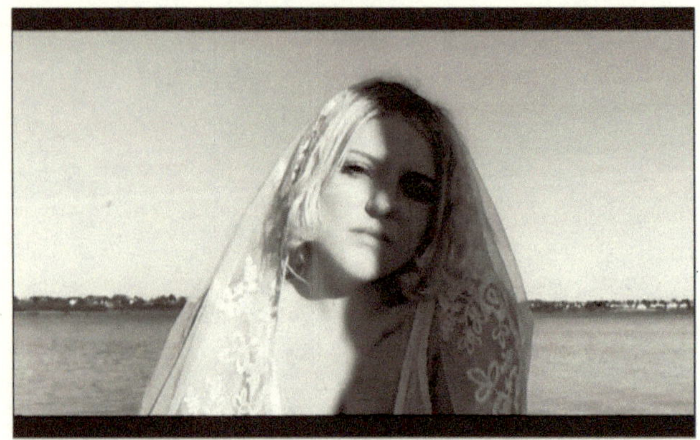

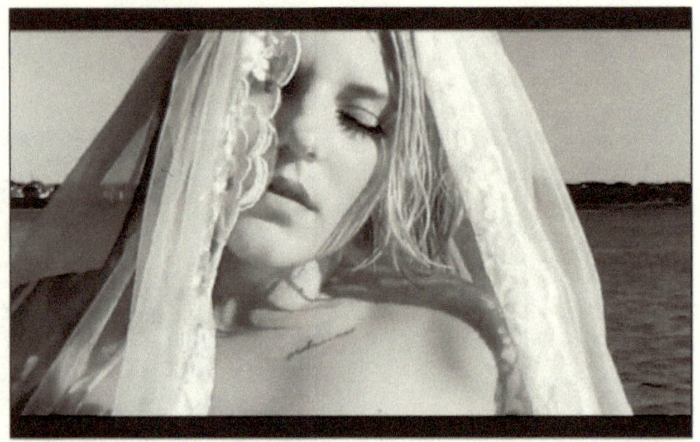

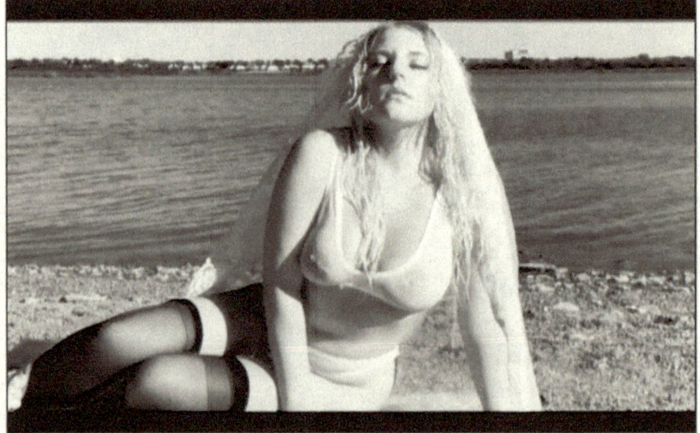

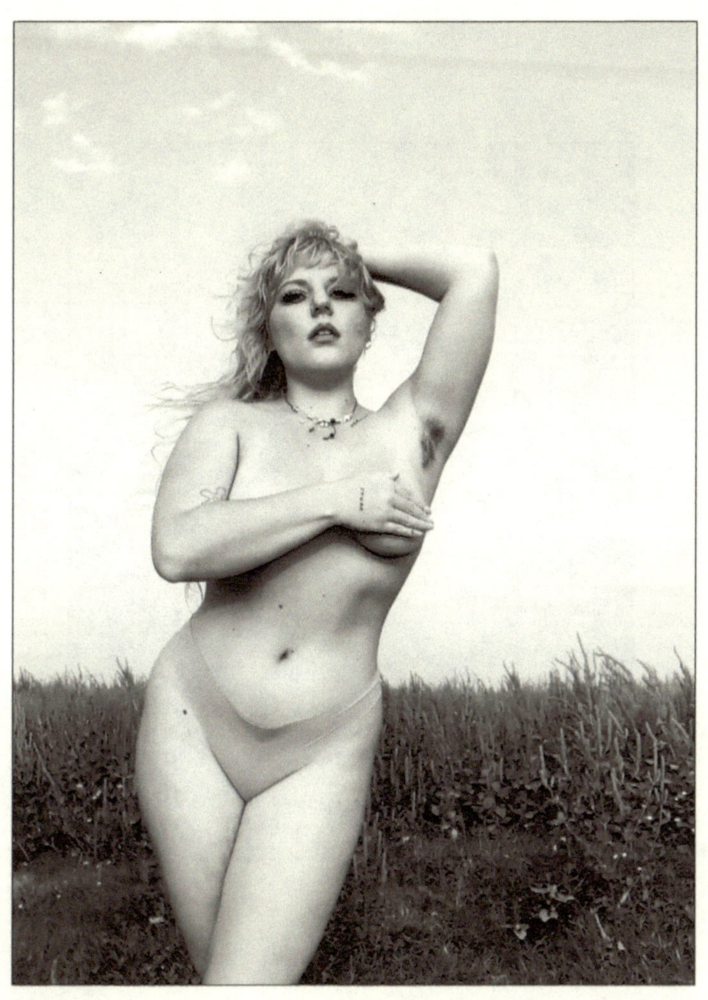

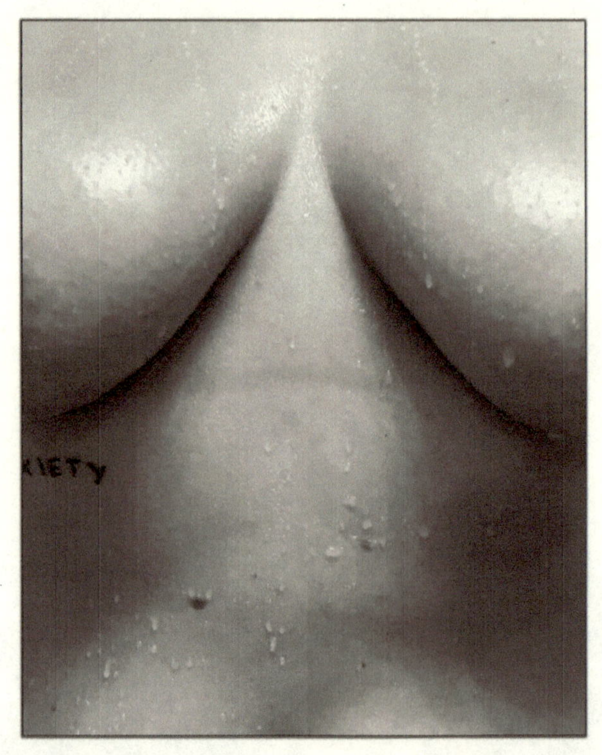

I WANT YOU

TO LOOK AT ME

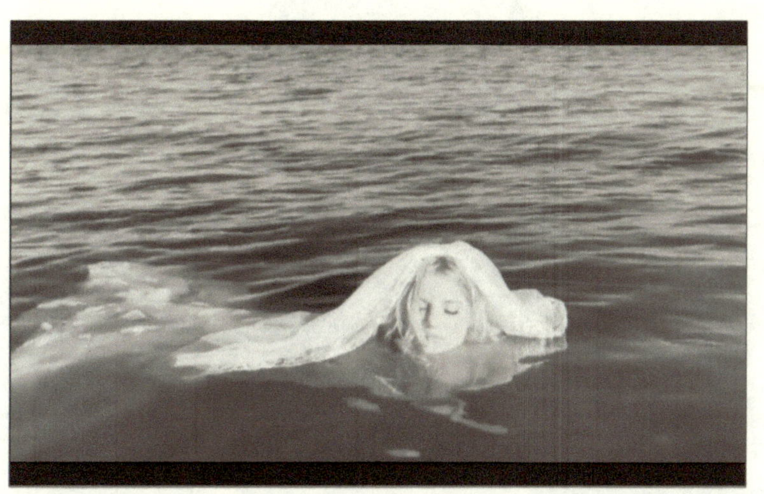

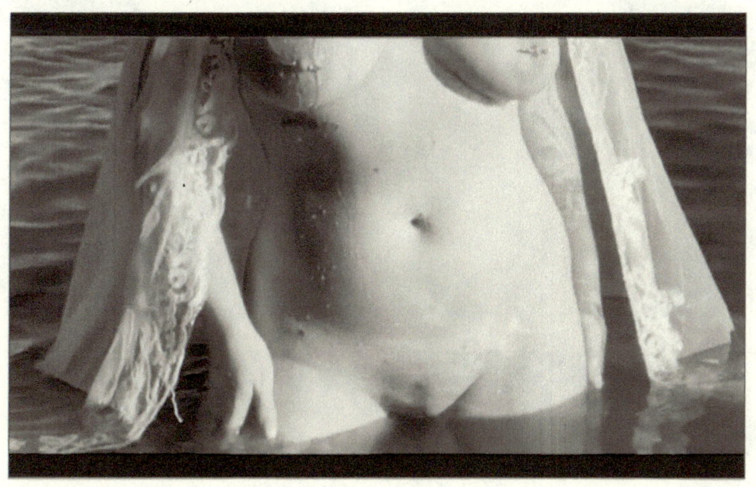

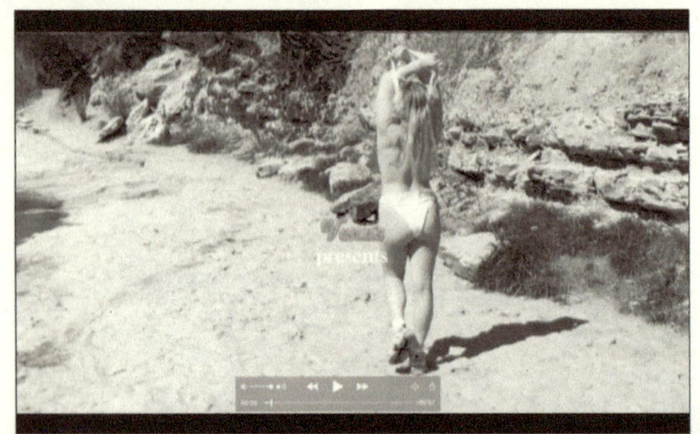
presents

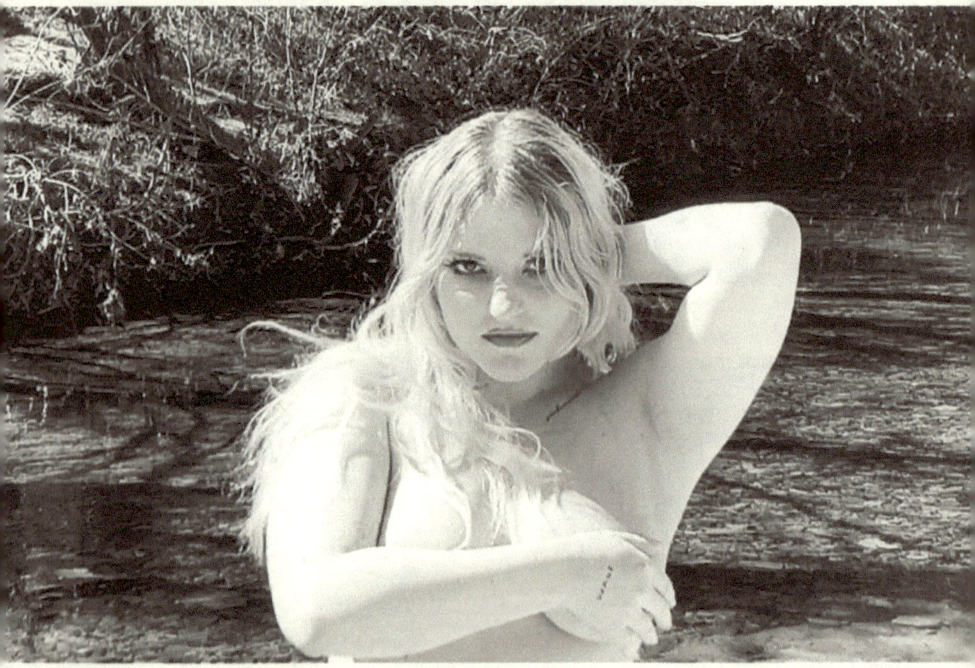

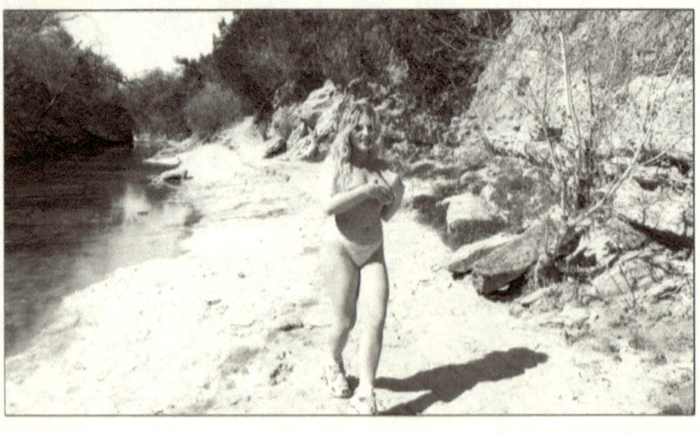

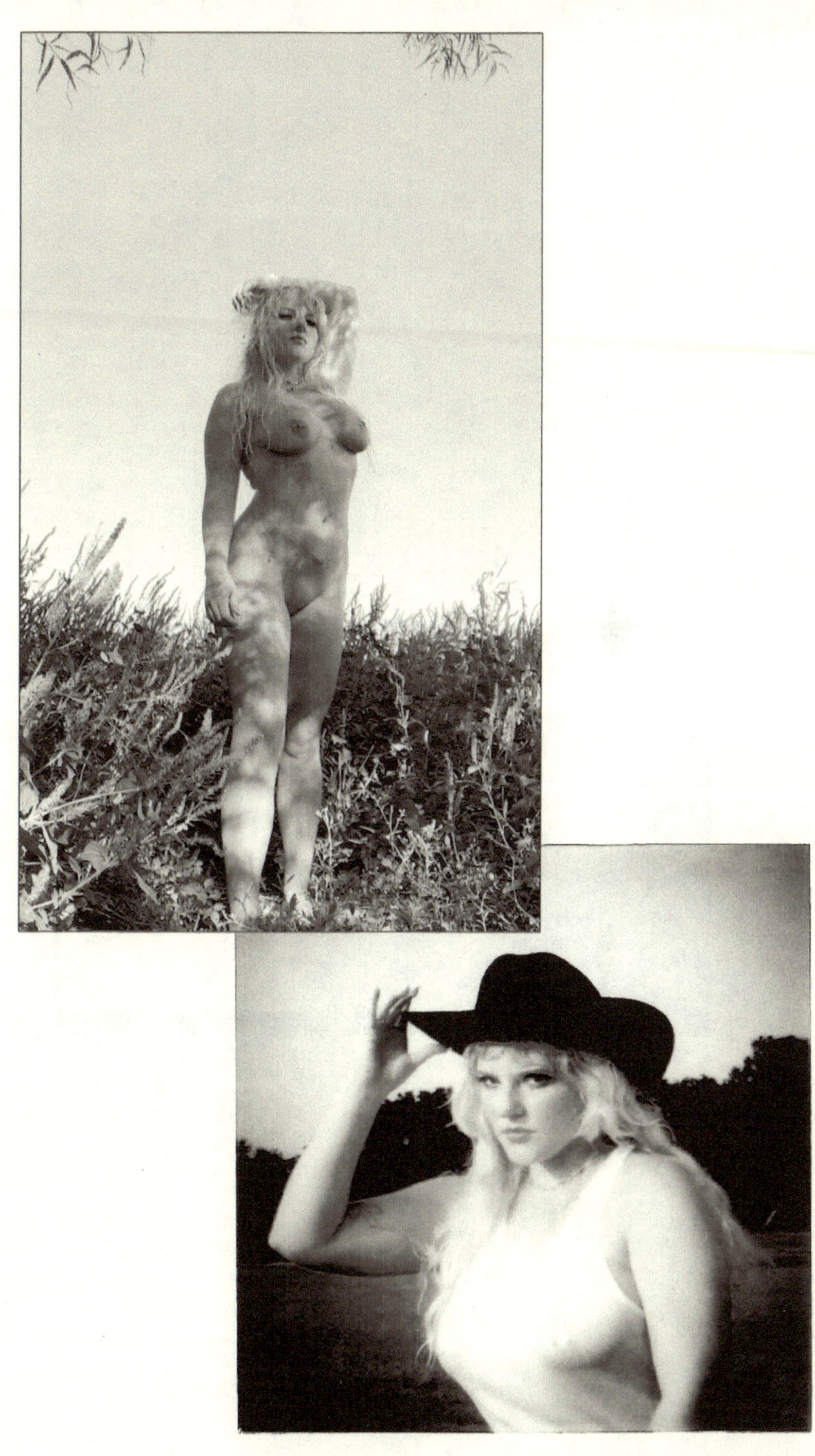

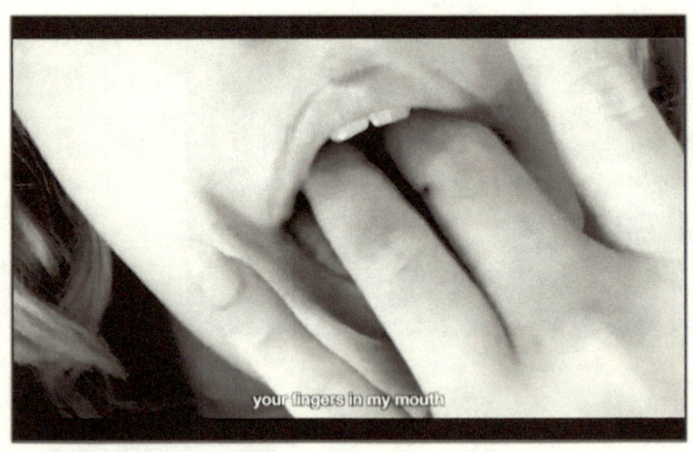
your fingers in my mouth

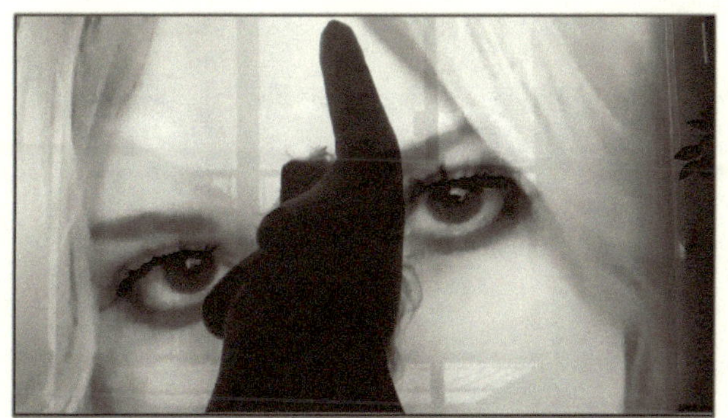

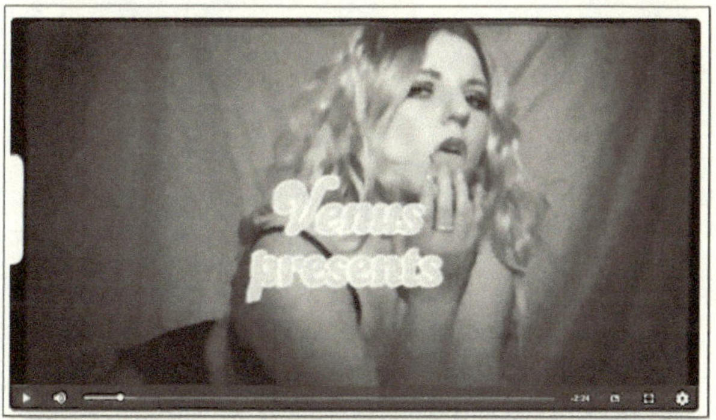
Venus
presents

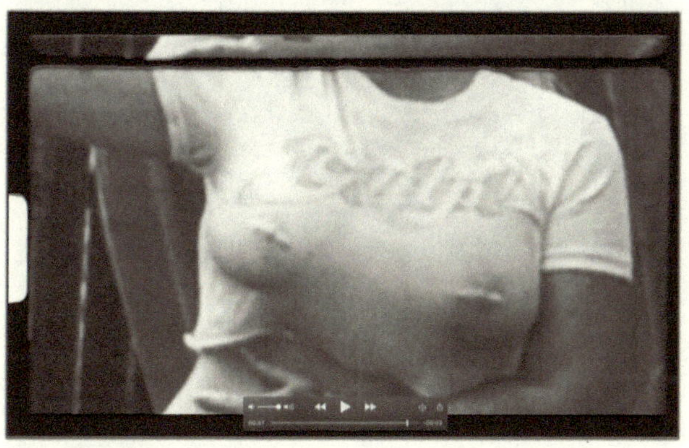

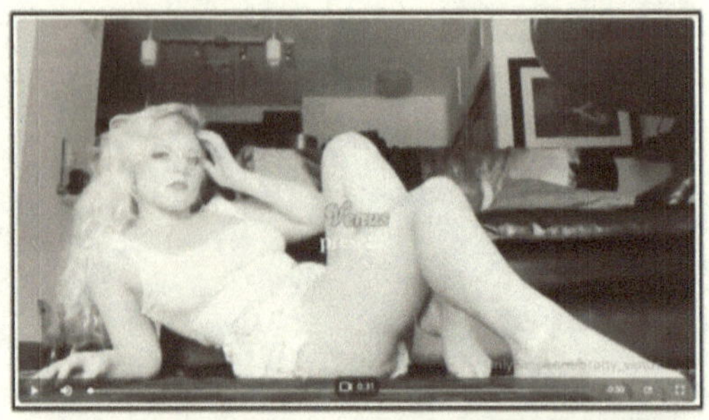

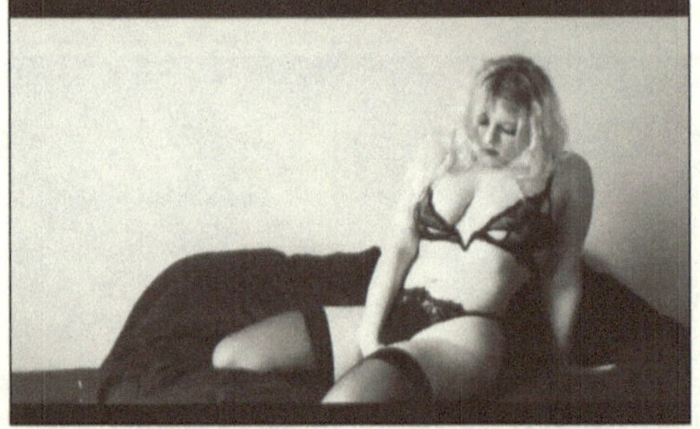

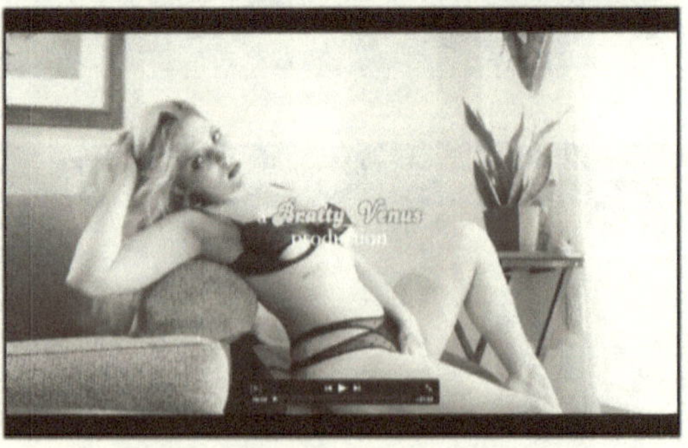

Hush, sweet Venus, for this is paradise
Whether you want it or not

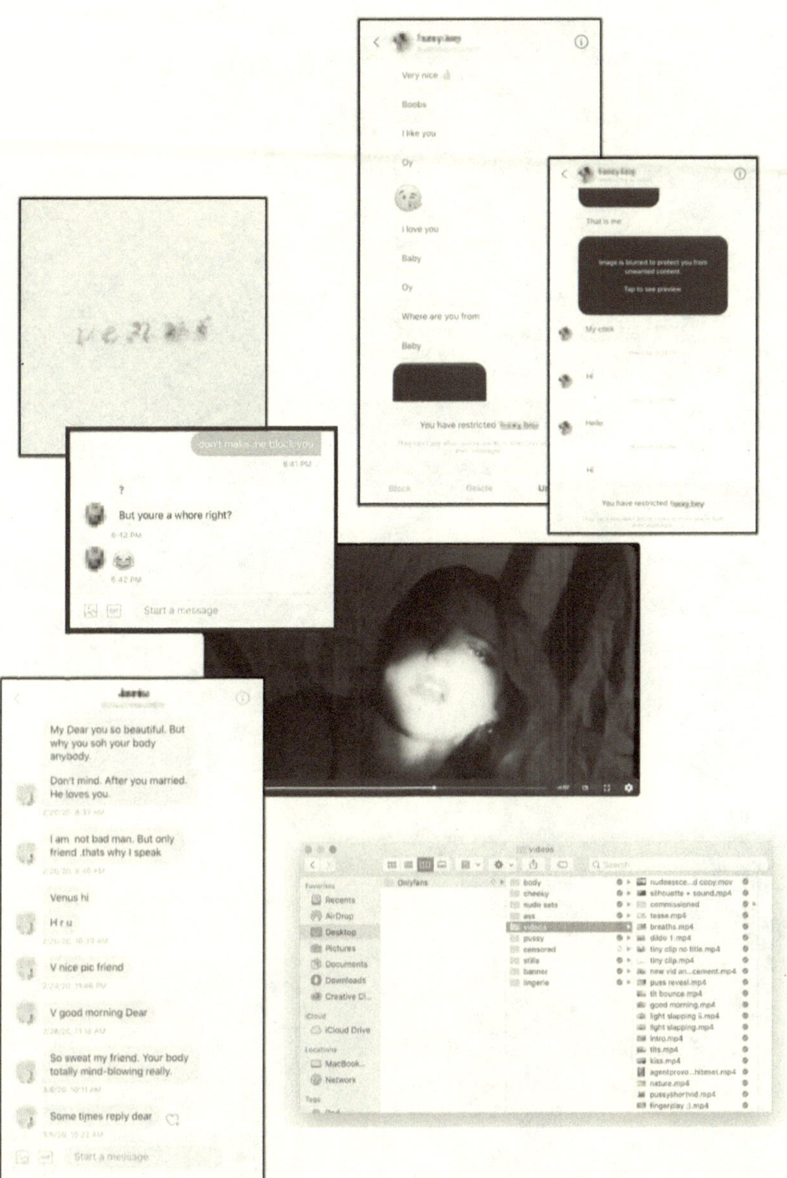

Very nice
Boobs
I like you
Oy
i love you
Baby
Oy
Where are you from
Baby
You have restricted
That is me
Image is blurred to protect you from unwanted content.
Tap to see preview
My cock
Hi
Hello
Hi
You have restricted
don't make me block you
?
But youre a whore right?
Start a message
My Dear you so beautiful. But why you soh your body anybody.
Don't mind. After you married. He loves you.
I am not bad man. But only friend .thats why I speak
Venus hi
H r u
V nice pic friend
V good morning Dear
So sweat my friend. Your body totally mind-blowing really.
Some times reply dear
Start a message
videos
Recents
AirDrop
Desktop
Pictures
Documents
Downloads
iCloud Drive
MacBook
Network
Onlyfans
body
cheeky
nude sets
ass
videos
pussy
censored
stills
banner
lingerie
silhouette + sound.mp4
commissioned
tease.mp4
breaths.mp4
dildo 1.mp4
tiny clip no title.mp4
tiny clip.mp4
puss reveal.mp4
tit bounce.mp4
good morning.mp4
light slapping ii.mp4
light slapping.mp4
intro.mp4
tits.mp4
kiss.mp4
nature.mp4
pussyshortvid.mp4
fingerplay :).mp4

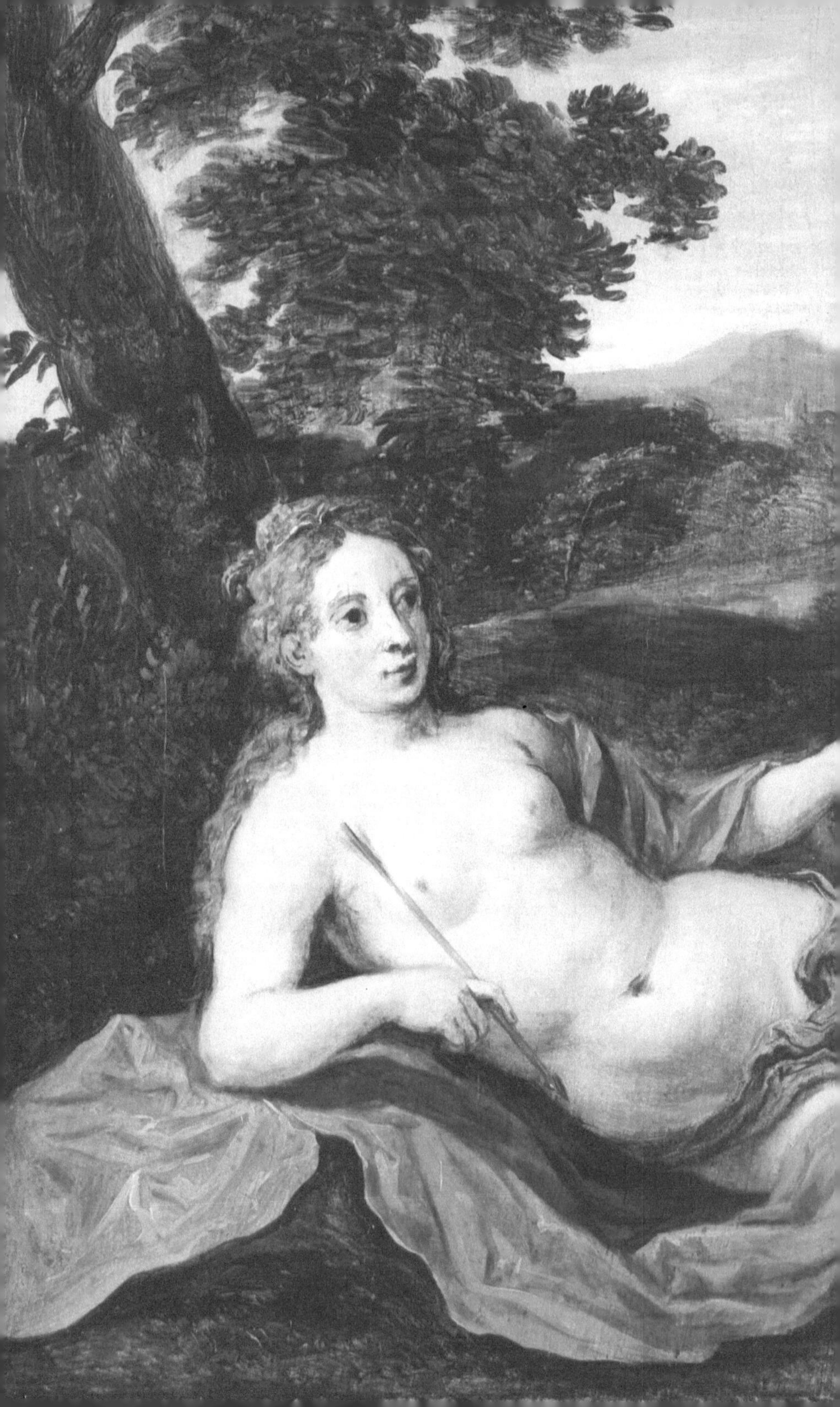

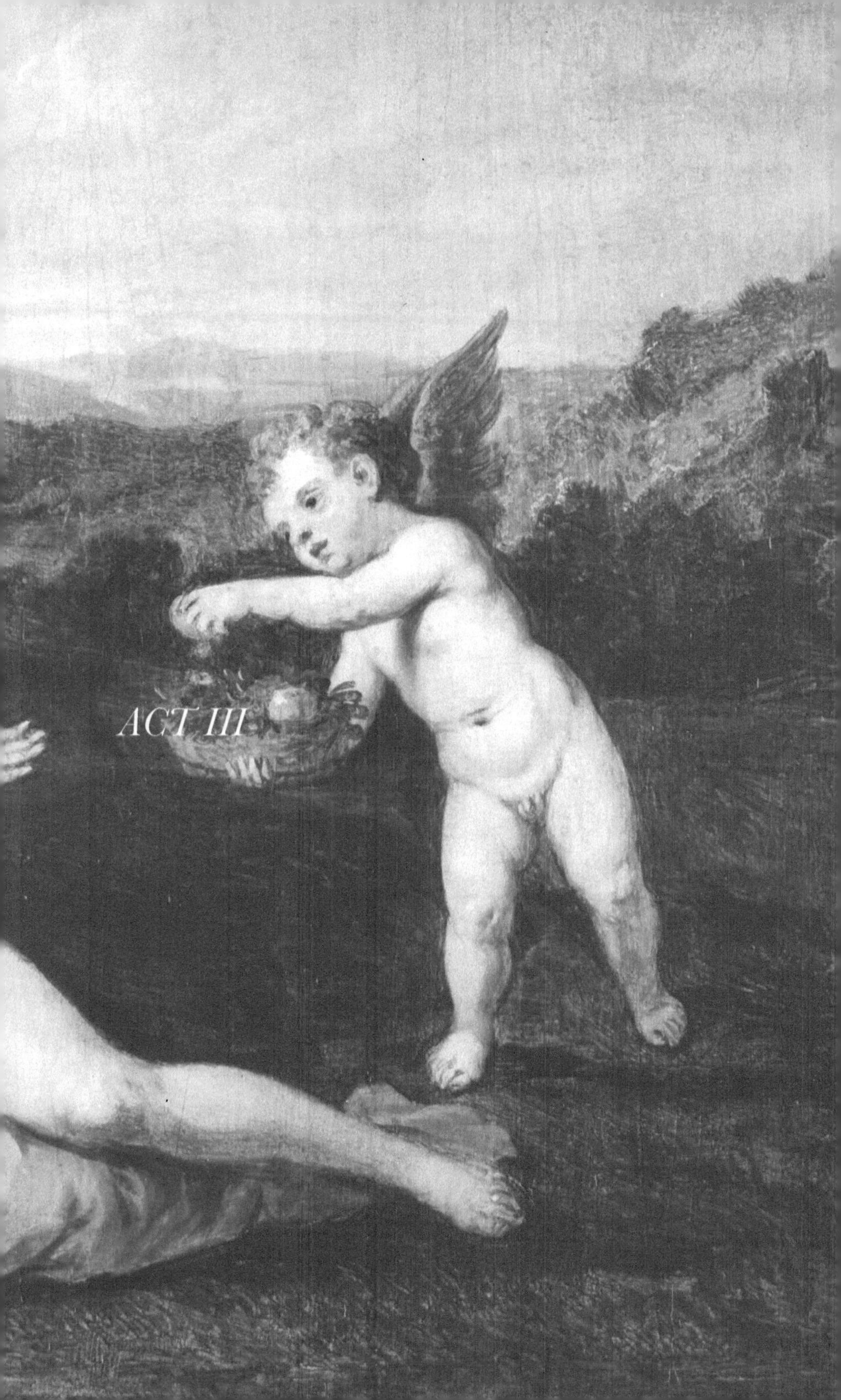
ACT III

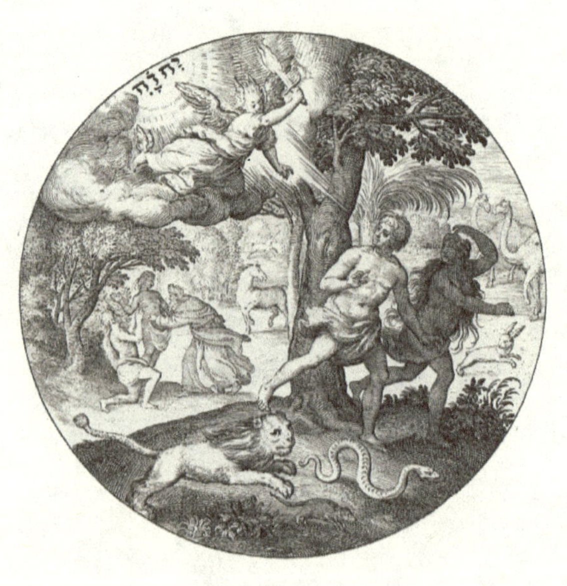
יהוה

Venus Reborn

I.

Venus, she dances in spotlights that never fade
Body wrapped up in chartreuse silk
Sea foam green goddess of earthly desires
Hedonist with so many children inside of her

Venus, clutching immortal pain
Fists forming hard pearls, each a memory
Of another hurt she wears close to her

Venus, sweet Venus,
Goddess of love with plump lips and soft thighs
Straddling gods who can't love her,
Stripping for drunk old men
Because she can't escape the spotlights

Sea foam green dollar bills
Venus with bruises on her knees
Venus forced to swallow the babies she so craves
Sea foam green eyes on the men who abuse her

II.

Venus is bedridden, she eats only fruits
And sets herself on fire when you touch her

Venus is calling in sick to work
Kiss your lovers while you can,
Venus, the goddess of tenderness is coughing up blood

Venus' eyes are red, there's never flush in her cheeks
She hides in long grasses and sleeps on ocean floors

Is Venus alive? She shakes the earth
And takes it down with her,
Ruby-red flame on her tongue
Is the last thing we see

III.

Venus sees a therapist on Tuesday mornings
And takes Prozac that wasn't prescribed to her
Venus—the sad sack, the crazy ex, the every woman
Venus, goddess of desire, can't orgasm on antidepressants

She drinks black coffee and wears black when she's sad
Venus, the former middle-school MySpace scene-queen
With black teased-up hair and cuts on her arms

She oversleeps and runs out the door with wet hair
Venus, sleepy Venus,
The goddess of fertility is going to get fired
If she can't stop yawning at work

She stuffs her body into a little black dress
Only to be ripped out of it when her lover gets home
Venus' boyfriend wants her on birth control
When Venus holds her cousin's babies,
Her uterus aches

IV.

Venus in blue jeans and blue mascara
Baby blue marabou wrapped round her neck
Venus—the angel, the Madonna
The whore with an empty womb

She resurrects urges, lets her body
Envelop new bodies
Venus, pussy wet with hope,
Still crying in the baby blue spotlight

Venus, the siren with a flytrap mouth
Selfish lover earning the right to be selfish
Baby blue silk sheets stuck to Venus' round ass
Perfume on pour, sweet baby Venus on tap

V.

Venus is a soft butch in feminine drag,
A beam of yellow light in a body belonging to everyone
But her

So she lets her hair grow longer,
Lines her lips and softens harsh facial features
With pinks and browns, powders and wax
Venus is afraid when she looks in the mirror

Saccharine Venus,
With charms sweet and venomous
Goddess of beauty who wears concealer and falsies
Changer of hearts, victor of war
Venus is on Tinder
Calling herself *queer* and trying to get laid
By someone who understands

She takes pills to sleep through the night
Yellow sunrise spotlights wake her up in lovers' beds,
Warm morning's glow on soft belly
Venus, the goddess of sex
Is trying to lose twenty pounds

VI.

Venus drives her friends to abortion clinics
And takes Plan B when the timing isn't right
She sleeps with women and feels protected
In a way no man has ever made her feel

She becomes a cam girl when her job turns sour
Bratty Venus, soft little slut of onlyfans and patreon
Shy financial dominatrix with a double life

She accepts Venmo and PayPal
And comes on command
Venus, the goddess of desire swipes her plastic
When she feels empty

She chokes on her throat chakra
And can't tell people how she feels in the daylight
When she's tired of crying,
Venus unfollows mothers on social media
No more smiling newborns imprinted in her brain
Safe baby Venus is secretly considering adopting

VII.

Venus is having nightmares about having nightmares,
She drinks citrus-infused water between each bad dream
And only sleeps well once the sun has started to rise

She wakes every morning
With an aching mind and heartbroken limbs,
Cayenne pepper and warm lemon imbedded into her morning breath

Venus is unable to keep track of days,
And has to write things down to embalm them—
To preserve the memories she can't retain
Without cheat sheets
Venus, the embodiment of all performative feminine drag,
Is taking lion's mane to try to remember

Venus walks parallel to the ocean,
Breathing in the salty air until she tastes home—
Her beginning and end, the birthplace of her every new life
Thrashing below an orange evening sky

She places expiration dates on every relationship
But falls half in love with anyone who doesn't hurt her
Venus, vulnerable little baby Venus,
Goddess born of the sea
Can't keep her head above water

VIII.

Venus is alone, shedding her uterine lining
To remind her of what she doesn't have

While her head pulses
With the heavy beat of her broken heart

She gets a shot of Depo-Provera
And can't stop thinking of suicide
But poor, sick Venus feels too weak to do anything about it

When a storm knocks out the power,
She sobs in a lukewarm bath
And drives, wet, through lightning so she doesn't have to be
Blue in the dark

She clings to her lovers,
Constantly apologizing for who she is
Venus, fucked up little Venus
Doesn't know how anyone could ever love her
Even when they tell her over and over again

Venus is an archetype, a concept, a mirage—
Everyone's fantasy, no one's true love
She's what everyone wants until the novelty fades
Men put her on a pedestal, but Venus always falls off

IX.

On lonely nights, Venus can still feel the sting
Of her past lives
Venus, poor, broken-hearted Venus
Doesn't know how to feel angry
So instead, she only hurts

She drinks four cups of coffee and paces around in circles
She cries with the doors closed, and pulls it together
When she has to
Venus' friends are afraid to let her drive home
Suicidal baby Venus,
Can't tell them not to worry
Without lying

Venus is a bruised and fuzzy little peach
When she cries, it starts to storm outside
To match the inside of her
When she looks in the mirror,
Venus sees cracks of lightning
When she hits her head against the wall,

She can hear the sound of hail
In the distance

Venus is a reincarnate, always alive
And tethered to the earth
Venus, goddess with Borderline Personality Disorder
Doesn't know how to get through the day
Without dying all over again

X.

Venus shivers where she used to sweat
She takes boxing classes and carries pepper-spray
In her purse
She wears only colors of the ocean
And gets tattoos in blue and green ink

Men on the Internet tell her she's desecrating her body
With each new word or drawing
Venus, the goddess of sex,
Trapped inside a body
Of which everyone thinks they have ownership

Venus wears soft lilac training sets
And lets people braid her hair before workouts
She chases endorphins, her lungs hot with sting
Practicing soreness as a healthy way of self-harm—
Pain as discipline, hurting as healing

Venus, made up of saltwater, with salty tears on her cheek
Venus with a mirror, cruel to her reflection
Venus feels phantom limbs touching her in empty rooms
Venus with unresolved daddy issues
Still haunting her after all these years

XI.

Venus falls asleep on Latigo Beach
And dreams of the same waves that lap at her feet—
That they do so just to sooth her,
Each ebb and flow a gentle touch of comfort,
A paramour whispering:
Venus, my love,
It will all be okay

Venus imagines herself sinking into the dense sands,
Deeper and deeper until she's finally free of the earth

Silly Venus, don't you know
Your deaths are only temporary?

Venus, the perfectionist, often covered in blood
Venus, wielding sharp knives and poisons
Venus, with skin of silk pressed into hot sand
She wakes up pink, but can't feel any pain

XII.
Venus is paralyzed,
Surrounded by statues and placed on display,
Carved from heavy stone
And left to feel tourists touch her bare breasts
As they pose with her for photos

Forced upon her is a hot white spotlight,
A captor she can never escape

Hush, sweet Venus,
For this is Paradise
Whether you want it or not

Indulgent baby Venus
Venus, the evening star
Venus, who must learn to show no mercy
Let Venus scream

Sold My Soul and Got Nothing to Show for It

I took an edible on Christmas Eve
And my dog ran away, came running
Back after an hour
I probably should've been mad
But I get it,
Sometimes you just have to get out

I spent New Year's Eve with four middle-aged lesbians,
A man who loved me, and a baby girl
Who played with her plastic charcuterie board
While we snacked on the real thing,
And wine kept appearing in my glass

The baby tripped over my boot
I asked if she was okay,
That little one-year-old told me
Yes, I can take care of myself
I wish I could say the same

New year, but it's all the same
Time isn't real and we're all in different time zones
So don't expect clocks to work like magic,
The stroke of midnight doesn't mean shit

Raise a glass for a cultural reset of so many false promises
To oneself, resolutions with no resolve
In a world that can't predict what's to come

New year, same old problems
Sold my soul and got nothing to show for it
Nothing left to lose when you're not where you want to be
Tattoo "Venus" on my hand, so maybe I'll remember

Welcome home,
But where is home when you don't belong anywhere?
Shakespeare wrote that the world is an oyster,
Sounds like bullshit to me

New year, but are we happy?
I forgot I'm supposed to be taking vitamin D,
No wonder cloudy days keep slapping me in the face,
Friday's warm tornados push in Saturday's snow

This $6 coffee tastes like shit but I'm exhausted,
So bottom's up
Drag me down the street, to the other side of it all
I wonder if I'm stupid
And bad and undeserving

Not a girl,
Just a color
Maybe not even a color,
Just a tint

The view from the outside, looking in
Ain't much better

On January 3rd I wrote a thousand words
But didn't feel like hitting "save,"
So that one was just for us,
No one will ever know

New year, same anxiety
There's no skin left inside my cheeks
I want to find a new therapist,
But having to explain myself all over again

Seems like a nightmare
It's probably the same reason I'm still single,
I just want you to already know me, you know?

In the middle of January
I fucked up my high heels in a mud pit, not the first time
Danced in the corner at Caves on a Wednesday
Dance floors always feel like fishbowls,
I don't want to be watched

Has creativity forsaken me?
Y'all, trust me, I'm more okay than I sound
I'm just tired of tired of it tired of it tired of it all
Every day is a blessing, or whatever shit people say

This January has lasted three months at least,
Downs and ups and downs even further
But at the end of it all
We've come a long way to get here

New year, clean start
No room left in my brain to remember names, or my childhood
But fuck if I don't remember that one time in 2004
I mispronounced the word *tenure*
Or when I said *orchard* but meant *orchid* in 2010

I can sing every track of Ashlee Simpson's *Autobiography*
So no, I'm not going to remember how to parallel park
Or the faces of people I met once, three months ago
Or when I'm supposed to get an oil change
Or the goddamn meaning of life

New year, new lobotomy
New grandiose ways of letting life
Roll off your shoulders
There is no space left between
Feeling nothing and feeling everything

In almost every dream I've ever had
The locks on doors don't work,
So I hold them tight in my hands
But people always get in
Anyway

Funny, how nightmares come to feel like progress
Because at least they mean
I slept long enough
To dream them up

New year, same old me
Selling shit no one wants
Writing books no one wants
Wanting so badly to be wanted
To be wanted

I love when people know me enough
To see right through me
And the permanent walls
I've painted to look pretty

To tell when tears are still 90 seconds from flowing
Because the clench in my jaw tightens ever so slightly,
The exact moment they somehow know to ask,
You good?

Oh, my friends with their strong wisdom
And their prophecies

Sometimes you just need someone to remind you
You're sick as fuck

OnlyFans/But You're a Whore, Right?

The boys who used to bother me
are paying to see me naked

This is all
some kind of perverse reparations

My mind continues to practice
how to forget

Art and commerce,
performance and smut

Where is the line?
and does it even matter?

Lost somewhere between the charismatic masochist
who begs to have my heels dug into his chest

And the arrogant prick who sent photos of his dick
and responded to my anger with *but you're a whore, right?*

Don't let anyone fool you
into thinking this is easy

Those leaks back in January
were all about control,

Toxic masculinity can't handle
when femmes finally set their own boundaries

(If you think I'm talking about you,
I'm probably talking about you)

What used to exist in the shadows
moves further into frame,

Spotlights on the sex workers
even though the clubs have emptied

That new verse in *Savage*
sends a shiver down my spine

Only a matter of time until everyone recognizes
that little blue icon on our phones

Overhears the name *OnlyFans*
and knows what it means

Until potential love interests find videos
in their pre-first-date internet searches

A modern-day scarlet letter
with an OnlyFans watermark in the corner

Split Ends and Smeared Mascara

My body is a seashell
I slide in and out of

When your head is on my chest,
Do you hear heartbeat?
Or ocean?

My internal white noise
A comforting lull,
A quiet routine
Of self-soothing

Morning light breaks thorough
A nostalgic bedroom,
Curtains pulled to welcome the day

I wake up to what already feels
Like a memory

Fever dreams, brain cut with a knife
Is this love a placeholder?
I already forgot

I want to protect you
I want to protect me

I'm sorry for writing about you
(You know you love it;
I know you hate it)

I never meant to be so sure
That one day I'll hurt you

I can handle it
So you said

You're good and pure
So you said

I don't want to change you
So you said

My little gay girl
So you said

But it still hurts
So you said

Don't cry
So you said

I know I'm being unfair
But you signed up for unfair

I'm no saint I'm no saint
I'll keep saying it
Until you hear me

Because even at my best,
I'm jealous and challenging,
Possessive and doubting

Even at my best
I'm needy and damaged,
Young and longing for someone who's not a man

And when this ends
I hope, somewhere buried deep down
You breathe a small sigh
Of relief

You say things that are deal breakers,
So why can't I just leave?

Tell me again
How hard it is to be a man right now

I thought I was strong enough to stick to my guns,
To choose head over heart
And say *fuck it* to nuance

I promise, I'm not writing this to invite tragedy

The love of my life is split ends and smeared mascara
Messy and tangled, flawed and human
Ugly even, from time to time

If it never stings, I forget it's so soothing
Every once in a while, I need you to break too

Stop stepping over broken glass
Just to get to me,
Careful with me in ways I never wanted

I'm no fragile clipped flower
Rotting through the stem

Venus enters Pisces
And I emerge from the shell,
Mouth sweet with banana and honey
With happy sleep and warmth
With hormones and vulnerability

The love of my life is more than survival
More than good
More than fine and rational

Can love be enough without ebb and flow?
Without storms after the calm?

You're just so goddamn level-headed!
Don't you want me yearning for your love?
Breaking down for your love?

Trying to be a straight girl for your love

Running out of patience
For your love

I wonder if I've given you all I have to give,
If I can't just tear off another piece of myself
To offer

Maybe I'll grow new organs to replace what's removed
Could I make you happy, then?

Am I strong enough to be the one
Who lets go first?
Hold on tight,
All I know is
I want to keep you a little longer

Surprise surprise
Miss indecisive changed her mind
Again

I love you
I love you not

I love you today
But what is tomorrow?

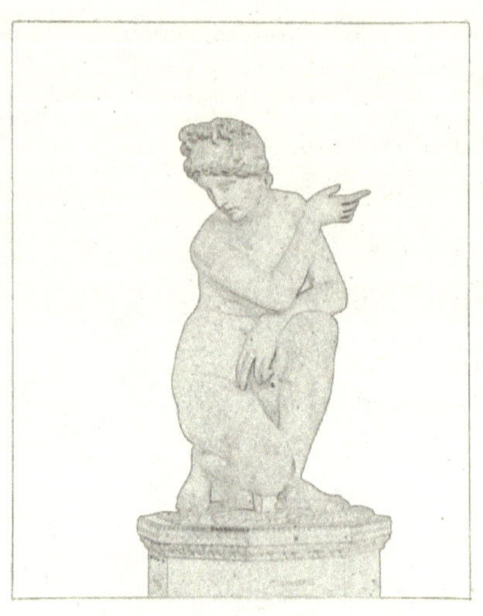

I am not a Poem

I'm worried I don't look young anymore. I can't commit to using eye cream. I can't commit to using my micro-current device. I moisturize my face, but can't remember to lotion my body. I've spent so much money on skincare over the years. I want my money back. I want my youth back. I want back the love I've wasted on undeserving vessels. Life feels less real every year. Everything is a cycle. We keep circling back to where we started. It's all just test after test, to see if we can close the loop how we were meant to. Third time's supposedly the charm? How many men have to fuck me over before I learn my lesson? No, I'm seriously asking you. I've gained weight in sadness; I've lost weight in sadness. I eat too much when I'm bored, so I try to stay busy. I don't always remember how to recognize my own face. I sometimes picture a child in my stomach. Not in a longing way, or even a curious way. More like, *damn my body really is capable of creating a life.* I don't remember signing up for that responsibility. I'm plump and ripe. My body feels full. My heart is only full on Thursdays and

Saturdays. I wonder how long we can sustain this. I can't keep holding your love hostage. Am I a bad person? I've never let myself be this selfish. My astrology app even says I'll be selfish in love today. Don't say I didn't warn you! I've never been one for *absence makes the heart grow fonder.* The less I see someone, the less I long for them. Maybe it's a glitch in my programming. I'm working on it. How old will I be by the time I pay off my credit cards? Is there even any point in trying? I have a "good" job and still can't afford rent. Twice minimum wage still isn't shit. Billionaires are literally hoarding wealth just so the rest of us stay deprived. How have we accepted this? Why didn't I just get another cash car after my last accident? I want a studio apartment, but when I live alone, no one knows when I spiral out of control. It's so much easier to be self-destructive when there's no one watching you. I should stop eating so much dairy. How do people learn to sleep through the night? How often should we *really* be using shampoo? Why can I only sleep with my hair soaking wet? How do I force myself to stay more hydrated? Drinking water that isn't ice-cold just feels like a waste, you know? I'm glad you don't try to fix me. I'm not looking for ways to leave, but I just don't know how long we can keep this up. It's going to be hard to go when it has to end. I sometimes feel existentially unfulfilled, even though everything is actually fine. I maybe want to quit my job (I definitely want to quit my job). How do you transition from a job to a career? They didn't teach us shit in school. I don't know how to do my taxes, but at least I'll always remember what mitosis is! I need to throw out the wilted tulips by my bedside. I don't have the heart to let them go. My pillowcase smells like sweat-covered nightmares. Wellbutrin exacerbates this, but I'll take the sweat stains and sleeplessness over constant thoughts of suicide. Is all of this worth not having to worry about getting pregnant? I feel like I haven't been okay since I got that fucking arm implant. How do you know if you're infertile? Is there an online quiz I can take? Babies sure are cute when they don't belong to you. I wish people would stop saying *you don't know that* when I say I never want kids. Like, no, seriously, I *really* never want kids. In some ways, being with women is so much easier. I'm tired of choosing between biting my tongue or teaching men things. Both are so emotionally taxing. Where are all the gay girls in this city? That one cute girl asked for my number at Havana, but then she left with her girlfriend. Is monogamy becoming too much to ask of someone? I know that's not the case, but it often feels like it. Is anybody *actually* okay? I sometimes still disassociate during sex. Does that ever go away? It's okay if it doesn't, I just want to know what I'm in for. It's still hard for me to have sex sober. I don't like knowing that about myself. A man at the gas pump next to me yesterday tried to tell me to get in his car and go get a drink with him. I spilled gasoline all over my new shoes, just to get away from him. I swear to god, if anyone says shit to me today, I'll fucking burst. I need to go back and re-read this book through my mother's eyes, through my partner's eyes. I'm not trying to break anyone's hearts. I'm still trying to write about other loves. The loves who fit me better, but always felt worse. The loves I shied away from when they wanted to commit to me. The loves I only clung to when they didn't want me enough. The loves who wanted me to dress more modest, to stop smiling at men, to pull my hair back. The loves who left with no explanation. The loves hiding porn addictions and texts to ex-girlfriends and saved photos of other women's tits on their phones. The loves who'd look into my eyes in broad daylight and tell confident lies, never a flinch in the side of their lip, never a twitch of the eyelid. The loves who controlled me, who admitted to molesting their younger sisters and made me hold them while they confessed to me wicked secrets I had nowhere to put (I was just a kid, too). The loves I knew, deep down, I would never learn to trust. The loves who never gave me a reason to. I'm trying to let go of the mistrust I've given a home in me. When I can't, I hate myself. When I can't, I swallow it deeper. When I can't, I shut my mouth, don't let myself hit *send*, say *yes, I'm okay*. When I can't, I put my phone on airplane mode and take deep breaths. When I can't, I open up internal wounds in an effort to release them, to make them bleed out, to relieve the pressure. I'm trying to let go of being misunderstood in childhood, of being dismissed as a stubborn girl, a bratty girl, a defiant girl for having panic attacks that looked like tantrums, for crippling separation-anxiety that looked like chosen neediness. I'm trying to let go of my father trying to drag me off to the psych ward in middle school instead of asking me what was wrong, to let go of my uncle kicking a hole in the bathroom door to try to get to me, to let go of the cops trying to figure out who to help. I'm trying to let go of quarter-memories I can't quite reach, but of which I can still feel the hurt. I'm trying to let go of being cheated on and force-fed lies, of the boys who made me think I was crazy rather than tell the truth. I'm trying to let go of boys who ignored my resistance, who took *no* as a teasing *yes* or just pretended not to hear, who entered my young body by force and whispered *I love you* right after, who made me say it back. I'm trying to let go of the confusions in me this caused, of my fear of long-term intimacy, of my reckless need to be loved and desired more than anyone could ever give me (again, I'm working on it). I hold grudges in my bones when I can't clench them in my head. How do you let go of the things that made you who you are? I'm trying to let go of these lasting resentments, of being so deliberately underpaid, unappreciated, and invisible. I breathe out and breathe in, trying to let out the grudges and only accept compassion. I'm trying to start each day anew. I'm trying to find a balance between being soft but not walked-over, of being kind but not enabling, of being confident but not controlling. I need to stop drinking caffeine just because it's something to do. I drink coffee just for the cup-to-mouth ritual, like how so many smokers say it's not about the nicotine. I can't be the only one, right? No one cared about my first book, and no one will care about this one. Am I even an artist anymore? Do words mean anything when no one reads them? Maybe I never had any talent to begin with. I'm tired of being called pretty by strangers when I'm just trying to exist. I'm tired of saying something dark and true and vulnerable and being told *well, at least you look good!* as if that's an okay thing to say to someone in a bad situation. I'm tired of wearing makeup. I don't owe anyone beauty. I don't owe anyone beauty I don't owe anyone beauty I don't owe anyone beauty! Why do I have to be so fascinated with glamor? I think I want to be a simple girl. Sometimes I'm just like… who the fuck am I? Is that normal? Does everyone think that? I miss you. I'm not supposed to miss you. You looked so cute this morning when you woke up and saw me next to you, writing a poem about sea foam in Los Angeles. I'm so terrified of you wanting to read this book. I always tell myself I can be hard on other people, as long as I'm also hard on myself. I'm no perfect protagonist. We all have our toxic tendencies we spend our lives unlearning. I need to get out of Texas. I think maybe I'm dying here. I sometimes feel like no one really knows me, even the people who know me best. I'm soft to the touch, hard to hold onto. You don't listen when I tell you *I am not a poem, so stop touching me in the ways you think I want to write about.* I think you always kind of wanted me to write about you. Last night you asked me if you were still in my book. I need other people to love, other people to love me. I feel like I have enough love to sell some off for profit. Am I strong enough to sell my affection? I'm still learning how to say the word *rape* aloud. I don't know what I'm doing with my life, I just know I don't want to move backward anymore. I've been putting off making a dentist appointment for twelve years. I often wonder how I'm still alive. I rallied after you accidentally fucked me in the ass. I take pride in monetizing off my sexuality. I'm learning quickly how not to shy away from my own body. I'm still broken, but I'm not as broken as before.

Spring Affair

In my early twenties,
Donna Summer's *Four Seasons of Love*
Narrates our orgasms, one for each season

Spring and summer as sweet as can be,
By fall I think I might be in over my head

I've put an expiration date on us, the way I always do
I just can't kick that bad habit
Of keeping an arm's length between myself
And anyone who tries to love me

But still, I cry with her when her head feels too heavy
I hold her in the mirror, make eye contact
With my self, admire how
Natural it feels to cradle her head against my body

Finger through her hair, my nails like a comb
Brushing the tangles out of her curls, the worries
Out of her mind, knowing I would do anything
To protect her

This is the only maternal I ever want to feel
We're both soft-bodied, gentle girls
With rough edges and emotional baggage
We've yet to unpack

I kiss her so sweet I can taste her soul,
Feel her tenderness falling into me
As much as I know how to let it

I'm always trying to get out before it turns sour
And fond, succulent memories rot and putrefy
(I'm only a control-freak when it comes to being loved)

She's such a vision with her hair pulled back,
Showing off the widow's peak
That she can't stand, but I can't help but find so sweet

I already feel a sting every time
I see one on another woman—
A soft foreshadowing of the bittersweet hurt I'll feel
When I remember her
After she's gone from me

I try not to let myself think about "someday,"
To just be present with her in every moment
Like every night is the last

She whispers something holy while I pretend to sleep,
So careful not to scare her with my hotheaded nightmares

When I can't be with her, my thoughts
Harmonize with one another
So I can feel less alone, less empty

I learn to think in her voice, to hear advice
Before she says it

The seasons change with us
Stars fall out of line

At some point, she stops texting
To see if I got home safe at night
Stops sending me songs that remind her of me
Stops laying her head in my lap on bad days

At some point, she stops introducing me to her friends
Peels my name off her tongue
Spits me out, back in my own bed

She asks how I can manage being
So warm and cold at the same time,
So deeply in love but with one foot holding open my doors,
So nurturing without being able to promise her tomorrow

Where do I go when I have nowhere to be? Alone
By my own design,
Desperately alone

It smells like lilies when she leaves,
Lingering in my senses even when I know
It must be gone

God grant me the serenity
To give my love without fear,
To be loved
To be loved again

Exquisite Odes

We spend an evening in August singing without words while we watch the sun rise on the turnpike for what feels like the last time—you can feel it in your fists, the sense of conclusion while we're switching back and forth between our personas, performing one more time to ourselves and one another
I wake up to watercolor daydreams that depict the lavish lives of humble beings, abundant in the ways of recurring lessons circling back until they've been properly heard by these souls, gently traveling, dripping with exquisite odes to life itself, and all of the experiences beyond compare, powerfully felt all upon different earths, different places of worship and devotion to exploring what life has to offer when awakened from a state of sedation, and delighted by the way we're all assembling in the spaces between life and the after—meeting parallel versions of ourselves, on different paths, bound by previous and future numbers and goals of learning and offering in a timeless unison—various pieces of momentum, continuous, but now running low on chances at redemption; humanity, still, clinging onto last-minute prayer—impulsive reckoning intertwined with thick visions of gods and their counterparts, planets and aspects and lines mapping our basic energies—burned into our eyes on the way to the next piece of existence, or nonexistence

Can we leave the earth?
Do we have a choice?

Chain-Smoking by the Pine Trees

(for Nancy and Amy)

Hospital beds become altars,
Each breath counted like a rosary bead

The air is heavy with reverberated echoes
Of a smoker's cough,
With worst-case scenarios,
With the fast-paced monotone reading
Of side effects at the end of a commercial

We pray around empty vessels
Holding on, just to let us offer
Our last goodbyes

Thank you for waiting

I chase my cousin's toddler around the halls
(The smell of baby skin
Drowning out the stale stench of death,
Whether real or imagined)
Holding this child with all the love I felt
For the woman who treated me like her own daughter

We clutch cold, pale hands with loved ones
Who've already left us,
Enter the room one by one,
Whisper *I love you*
And apologize

I'm still sorry I don't know
How to properly grieve,
I'll cry later
In inappropriate places,
But not here

Tell my boss
I'm calling in sad to work,
No tears on the sales floor
Even when it's life or death

No one sleeps for three days; comfort food has no taste
I drive twenty hours straight to get here in time,
And still can't fall asleep after

Did you know you can actually
Cry out your contacts?

My memories fade,
Pine-needle baskets turned to ashtrays

At least that coat still has your name stitched into it,
My foot reads *fuck cancer* in both of your honors

We vow to give up our unhealthy vices,
As if any of these things are so easy

We gather for warmth, exchange stories
Around a winter fire,
Take a shot or pour one out
For our departed aunts, sisters, daughters

We hear things for the first time,
The private stories and secrets
We took to their graves, but not ours,
Soak in a sense of bonding
All too late

Funny how you sometimes know people better
After they're dead

Didn't Anyone Tell You the Amazon is on Fire?

my lips are wet with another sip
to regret in the morning

nights were never meant for clarity
oh, but the daytime is sobering to a point of madness

I'm lost and dumb,
a brittle kid with two broken wings,
somehow born with no sense of direction

where did all that so-called promise
end up? what ever happened to
undying hope?

we used to believe in
so little and so much

depressions creep in,
hit me hard
until my brain has no room
for muscle memory

I try explaining to loved ones
how depression and unhappiness aren't the same

that the chemicals in my dumb idiot brain are off
and that doesn't mean anything concrete,
doesn't mean everyone isn't trying
hard enough

but poems begin to almost double as suicide notes
and I start to think in my head
when I say casual goodbyes
in case this is the last time you ever see me

I can't keep crying while I'm flying down the highway,
didn't anyone tell you the Amazon is on fire?

my childish hurting should feel smaller
when our lungs are burning,
it's selfish to feel burnt out
when the world is in flames

I know this

we lose our jobs one by one,
and it hits worse every time

we watch a lesbian love film
while we lose our health insurance—
gentle and poetic and tender and numbing

Summer hits different than when I played it on flute
queer longing is queer longing, no matter the century
to be drawn like one of your French girls always ends in tragedy
I'm still crying over page 28

we consume news
in sound bites and headlines

everything feels final,
we've made ourselves unsustainable

I try so hard
to leave nothing unsaid

by April, we're living in
another kind of world

in these moments we learn
whether we really fear death,
whether we even have it in us anymore
to flinch at tens of thousands of deaths

I wonder how anyone
has children anymore

there is no passage of time
with the curtains drawn,
it is always night
it is always day

never another alarm in the morning,
sleep too much
but also don't sleep at all

life is but a dream
is but a dream within a dream
is but a dream a little dream
is but a waking nightmare

I find myself swaddled,
my own warmth, my only comfort,
whispering conversations with myself
and the earth

do you remember the slower times?
of being born, of taking, surviving
before learning to give?
of earth, grass and soil, hands and knees

so far back, when every touch felt red-hot and electric
now turned to lonely in the suburbs
absent from touch, but our own

what made us capable of life?

did our parents ever wonder
what world would be left for us?
were our parents ever prepared
to love queer offspring?

were we meant to weep at the feet
of early morning's light
and pray for the earth's patience?
were we meant to sacrifice our loved ones
in the name of the dow jones?
was the earth prepared to die with us?

something is crawling
either on or inside me,
and that chill in my bones
can't tell the difference

but oh, my love,
such is life

if there is an end to this,
please let it be light

Gardenia

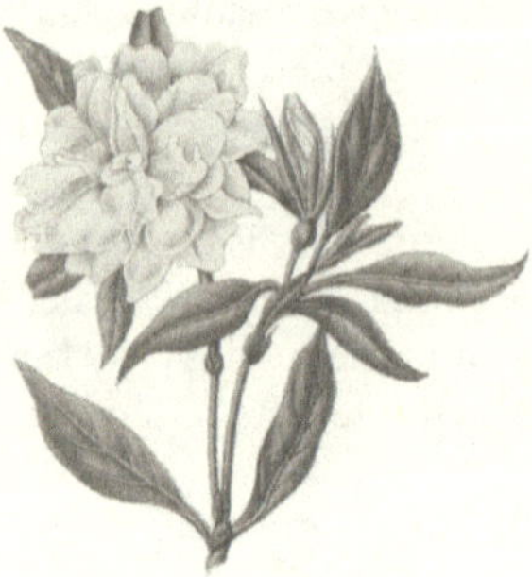

oh, she is resilient, like the people I've come to know with the summer speckled on our shoulders, and all across the roads to nowhere, or to somewhere fixed between holiness and damnation, with intense visitations from both—the wild gardenias and thorn-covered vines; the sweet young rabbits and the bitter rattlesnakes, on the road with us, searching far and wide for some kind of salvation through bright moments caught on film, and white sands clinging to sweating skin in New Mexico against quiet mountains mirroring curves of the human condition

are we all playing house? with sliding doors and spiral staircases up to rooftop gardens with views to everywhere? breathing in the air, so saturated, and watching sharp stars and their connections to one another? how many nights can be spent driving down the main drag, through all of these places that don't belong to us? camera batteries rattling on the floor of the car on wet roads in San Antonio, girls laughing, barefoot in filthy rest stops wearing beautiful, hand-made, green velvet clothing with subtle flowers quilted into their design, leaning against colorful mosaics of cowboys who loudly and ironically remind us of where we are—embedded into the wide Texas middle of nowhere, chasing the desert and singing along to the pop songs of our youth, *hit me baby one more time*, shadows of wild trees speeding across our windshield, reflecting endless skies and arms outstretched toward them, us, breathing in the ghosts who walked here before us

I miss my friends; I miss my childhood with endless possibility and so much energy to create (isn't it funny how we misremember?)

did I leave behind my motivation in the mountains?

by the Skin of our Teeth

Time is a funny thing,
Stars dance and laugh around us

Another Mercury in Retrograde
To get through
By the skin of our teeth

Rain taps against the windows
Like a transient visitor

Ashes to ashes
Show me how vast
My negative space can be,
Show me how much
Nothingness
I can swallow

My job disappears,
Health insurance runs out

In my spine
Is a gathering of rage,
I act to remove
The vertebrae's built-up temper

Dry skin begins to rip at the seams,
Sliver-cuts on the hands
Of an insomniac with no company
But the storms that hide the sunrise

Migraines and depression
Float back to the surface,
Bob up and down on water
And reflect the harsh skies

My rock, once unmovable,
Begins to crack

Awakened by nightmares,
Bad dreams mine and yours,
I blow out a candle
And think of you

No more twisted flames
Burning in the daytime,
Smoke one last cigarette in honor of
Your father, dead in New York

Your ex was in your apartment until 2am,
I'm not allowed to be jealous
Because two people are dead

I know you always do the right thing,
But sometimes the right thing
Still gets under my skin

Both our lips wet with whiskey,
I pick fights so that you'll fight for me—
Your selfish bitch, your greedy brat

I need to be the love of your life
Even if you can't be mine

(Call it hormones or stress
Or not taking my antidepressants)

I feel cruel for wanting you

Because I know I don't *need* you

You're the one who wrapped yourself
Around my little finger

If I say your name three times
You'll appear

I'm so well-versed
In self-sabotage

Writing Nicorette poems,
Little manic cinnamon couplets

What must it be like
To live on our tongues?

An aftertaste of unspoken words
Inhaled like salty ocean's air

Is each poem a knife?
Show me your back
And I'll kiss each stanza,
Taste the iron in
My every loaded word

Am I still pretty
When I'm mean?

I act crazy
And do the dishes
And fuck you senseless
So you forget

Thunder keeps me up,
Electric thrusts in the night

Remind me what it feels like
To be fisted

I become a performance piece
My body and limbs breathe in and out, wilt and bloom, wilt
And bloom

The breaths and hands and sunlight and pulsing pussy,
The lips and words and curves and motion

Through my curated commerce for the male gaze
I accidentally learn to love myself

Please, don't let this be the thing
That tears us apart

Secondhand Sins

hot girl summer, lobotomy winter
let's not solve problems that don't exist,
focus on the ones around us

the amazon is on fire
california is on fire
australia is on fire
my mind and body are on fire
the girls before me were on fire

and I can't put any of them out

how do we repent
for all of our secondhand sins? the residual
unconfessed vices, and the actions performed in the name of those vices

silence—the love child of trepidation and cowardice,
sweet little souls as the driving forces, the airs rising
every time we die,
every time we're bearing witness to the pains we can't heal

tattooing over cigarette burns and wondering why
we still feel the urge to abuse ourselves
when there's no one doing it for us

can we be stronger than the desire?
walk across bridges or rooftops of tall buildings
without the thought of jumping off?
do we risk standing too close?

if I say three hail marys for Eve
can we un-bite the fruit?

all my life I've been witness
to women's strength to endure—
smile and endure
give all you can and endure
say thank you and endure
say nothing, and endure

how long do I have to go on enduring?
to how much more am I expected to submit?
I'm not getting any younger

the earth caves in on us,
it's unsafe to go outdoors

these are the plagues
we never thought would come

don't listen to the president
to the pedophiles
to the rapists and power-hungry monsters wearing masks
of wrinkled white flesh and disarming business suits
hell hath no fury

we let go of our manipulative tendencies,
push them off the edge
when they're dangling out open windows

my mouth is small
my mouth is tense
my mouth is shut,

teeth marks in my bottom lip
from holding them closed,
from eating my words

how do we dismantle what's happening around us
in order to save what's left?

the seasons are changing outside without us,
and now we've always got escape plans

Impermanence

Too drained to put fresh sheets on my bed
I lie awake on my stained mattress,
Flowers and ivy and sweat and blood

The wall politely asks that I stop staring at it,
Calls me *voyeur* even though I gaze through it,
Never at

Cursed with gluttony as my vice
I thrive in excess, in too much

In such nothingness,
I unravel

Sit in the calmest mania from the outside looking in,
Devour the insides of my mouth
Until there's nothing left to chew,
Drain my bank account
While stressing about the consequence

Tell people online to look at me,
Glorify me

Touch yourself to my videos,
Does it feel like I'm here with you?

Tell me how badly you need to fuck me right now
And I'll disappear

Desire can only get you so far,
Pretend I am forever
And I will show you
My impermanence

I water my poems,
Soft bouquets turn to gardens
Overgrown, they obscure windows
And light, pathways in and out

Cut on the thorns of my own long vines of tenderness
Love, unattended to
Turns sharp around me

I bleed out my urge
For melodrama

Sometimes my words
are too thick to see through

I'm Sorry Your Girlfriend is a Poet Who Poses Naked on the Internet

I'm sorry your girlfriend is a poet
who poses naked on the Internet

Who makes a spectacle of small problems
and makes a spectacle of herself

Who writes about the worst of you
and wants her body to be looked at

Girl, made up of sex toys
and lingerie

Cunt pulsing in the sunlight
for $9.95

I'm sorry your girlfriend shows you nudes
That other men have already purchased

What was once meant for you, sent out
in a locked message to each of her subscribers

Anonymous icons get their dicks hard
and slide into her dm's

Sweet words flow from her heart-shaped face
as men pray over her heart-shaped ass

This jealous girl, too cruel sometimes
to understand why you don't like it

She'll be lucky to never let her get a taste
of her own potent medicine

Girl, made up of doubt
and self-loathing

Girl, made up of tears
in the night

I'm sorry your girlfriend is needy
without offering commitment

An almost-lesbian, she gets drunk and tells you
how hard it is for her to love you

Girl, made up of fear
of being alone

She'll wear you against her skin
until you've fully tarnished

Golds and silvers turned to a green
she can't easily rub off

I'm sorry you fucked up and fell in love with a writer
who has to sacrifice kindness for the most powerful stanza

Bullshit poems she'll no longer read you,
don't let her love go bad

Dallas

sweating tourists are taking selfies where JFK was shot
paying money to park in the city of old money and oil tycoons who collect art to seem relatable
and down to earth and "one of us" while the homeless roam the streets of Downtown
trying not to burn to death in the summer heat surrounded by empty upscale hotel rooms in these once-historic buildings

Fair Park becomes State Fair, gates open with mutters of *remember when Big Tex caught on fire?* asked between bites of deep-fried everything and sips of large frozen daiquiris on the land that once welcomed a special day for the KKK

there are bubbles of fresh spit on every sidewalk, glistening in the light of the sun or bright signs,
streetlights or cars in the night as another "entrepreneur" leans out the window
of his shining Mercedes and leaves his fluids on the pavement just because he can,

and raises his windows when he passes the religious men who gather on Fridays and Saturdays to scream across Main Street through a megaphone to tell us we're going to hell, to get on our knees and fucking repent

it seems like once a week there's another shooting in Downtown that
we only know about because the roads are closed
breaking news: an inconvenience leaves cars backed up down Commerce to I-30 and people honk their horns and curse and yell through car windows because we're so goddamn desensitized
and we can't help it

shining tall buildings reflect the sun into my eyes
people on the street will touch you without asking
I can't walk a block without someone yelling something at me
we're all just streetwalking sirens catching harassment in our big hair, avoiding eye contact with men
because give them an inch, they'll take the entire state of Texas
I forget my perspiring body is made of honey

even in the gayborhood being a woman means being a spectacle
fuck that one guy who tried to finger me on the dance floor at S4
and the guy who pressed himself against me while I was kissing a cute girl
and the white cis gay boys who call girls bitches
and only stan queens if they don't take hormones
and hate lesbians because they only want a woman around if she's fuckable
(it doesn't matter that they don't want to do the fucking)

capitalism spends June in rainbow drag using thin, white bodies to sell, sell, sell! in the windows,
fast and high-end fashion both donning their *#PRIDE* decals,
an empty gesture, no action

this is Hallmark
is Susan G Komen
is a wolf in sheep's clothing
is the same old slow burn bait and switch

it rained on the Pride parade but I didn't notice, moved from Cedar Springs to Fair Park
I heard they're charging admission

what would Marsha and Silvia and Stormé say if they saw the cops all
around us? abusive allies for hire, as if we've forgotten our own history

capitalism is a sugar baby feeding off our need to feel loved, to feel
seen,
but come July she's moved on
to red white and blue
star-spangled banners
if she sees us on the street, she'll pretend she never knew us

they say there are sixteen lesbian bars left in America,
so send my love to Sue Ellen's
and lesbian happy hour
and lesbian poetry open-mic nights I never quite made it to

there are makeshift homes beneath every overpass
ghosts of my past life roam the halls of this city
once remembered as *the City of Hate*
this was meant to be a love letter

August

my heart breaks a few times a day

walls close in
but it's okay as long I paint them

my to-do list just says
rewire my brain

DBT feels like a nuisance
not a solution

but I'll keep doing it so at least I can say
I'm doing *something*

I killed a fern
but at least my basil is thriving

I get harassed just as much
with half my face covered

maybe more

still, I tether my self-worth
to my fuckability

tie it all up
in tight triple knots

I sometimes think if no one is yearning for me
I might disappear

my therapist confirmed
I have borderline personality disorder

they also said
I don't like that one

I don't hate my body rolls so much
if I imagine I'm a painting
or a sculpture, something intentional

I've been here before
another rodeo for the books
I'll rip apart and throw away

my life might be a lot different
if I was a rich kid who played violin

I still can't remember
most of my childhood

I wonder if high school will still hurt
when I'm thirty

volcanic anger erupts from nowhere
burns us both
and I spend weeks clearing the ash

I know you said
for what it's worth
but babe, it isn't worth a damn

were you thinking of me too?
going through the archive
in your mind
of all the dirty things you ever did to me?

I swear, I almost felt you here with me

forgive me for trying
to fuck away the pain

it usually works
for a minute

the end came and went,
and we kept living anyway

Pomegranate

Dripping like a pomegranate in the early spring
your baby Venus,
exhibitionist with a shy streak,
brat in Agent Provocateur

Desires to be seen but never looked at,
to be touched, but never too soon
to be bruised when the time is right,
soft bite marks in the skin

Let me be ripe,
morning dew glimmering
like tear-stained cheeks personified,
like something once-bathed in holy water
does the pomegranate fall oh so far from the tree

Passions rise to the surface,
pink seeds burst with sweet
and melt on your tongue,
messy and fervent, soft and violent
red and red and brighter red

What a pleasure to hear the sound
of each seed as she explodes

There is such holiness in being unholy

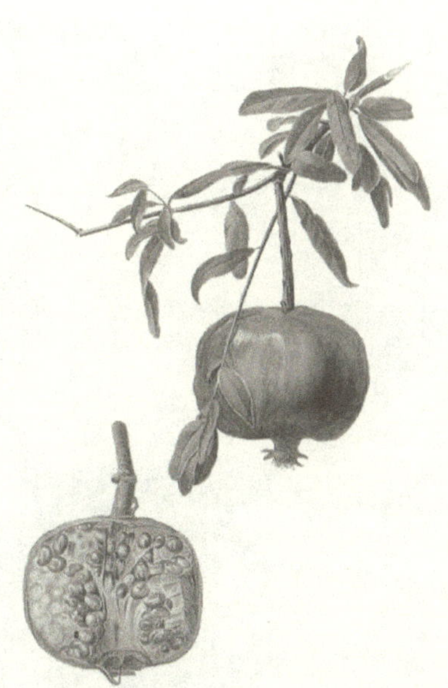

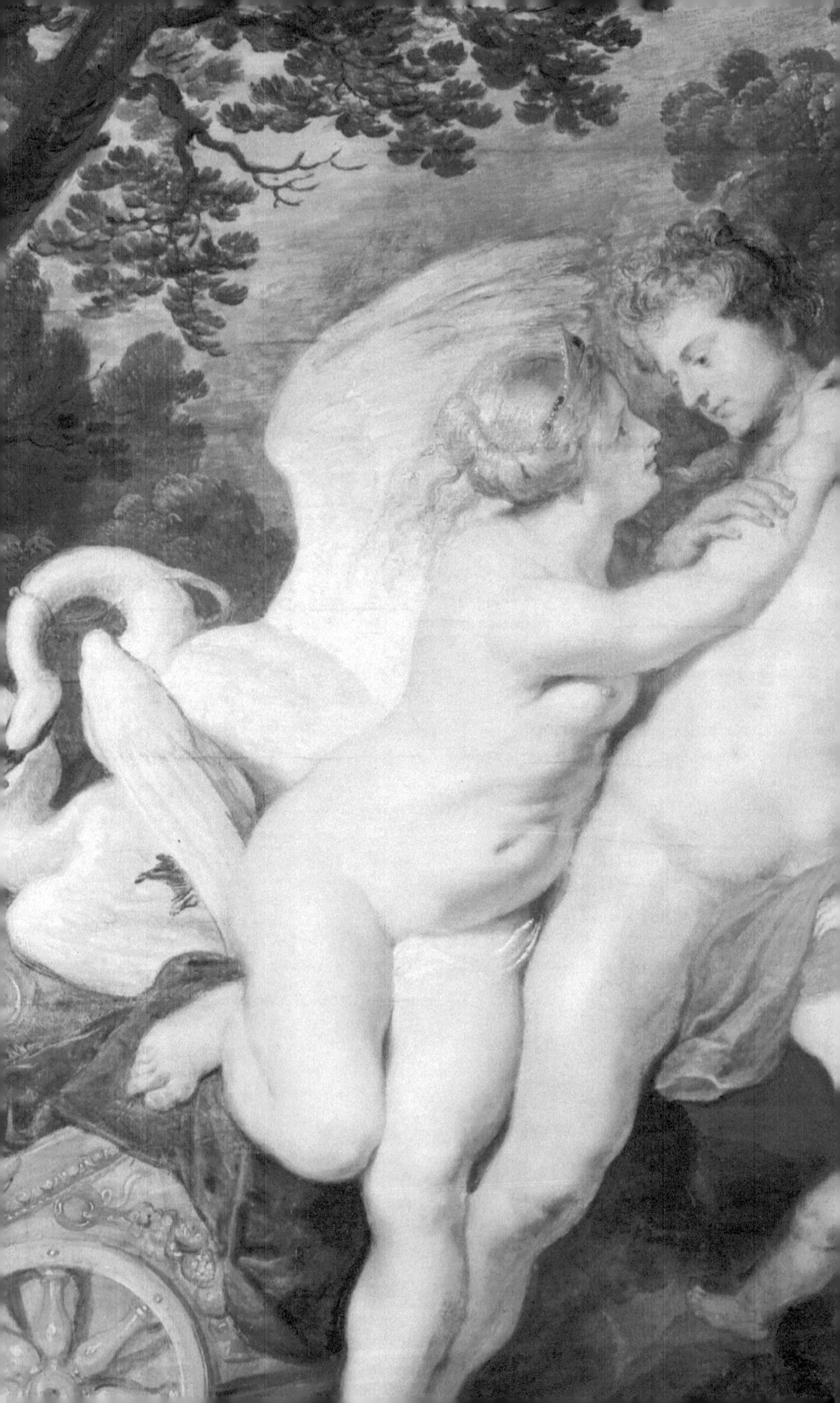

A special thank you to the generous contributors
who helped make this project possible:
(listed in chronological order of contribution)

Vicki J. Sapp
Crystal Garrett-McEwen
Austin Bachlor
Carlos Bachlor
Wendy Cho
Anonymous
Erin Johnson
Anonymous
Jennifer Schneider
Frederick W. Holston
Maddie Wehrmann
Anonymous
Flora Kirby
Katie Hitt
Georgina Martinez
Pierre Krausse
Jace Bachman
Charlette Hwang
Sabine Fletcher
Ethan Christensen
Natalie Sizemore
Dimaggio Escobedo

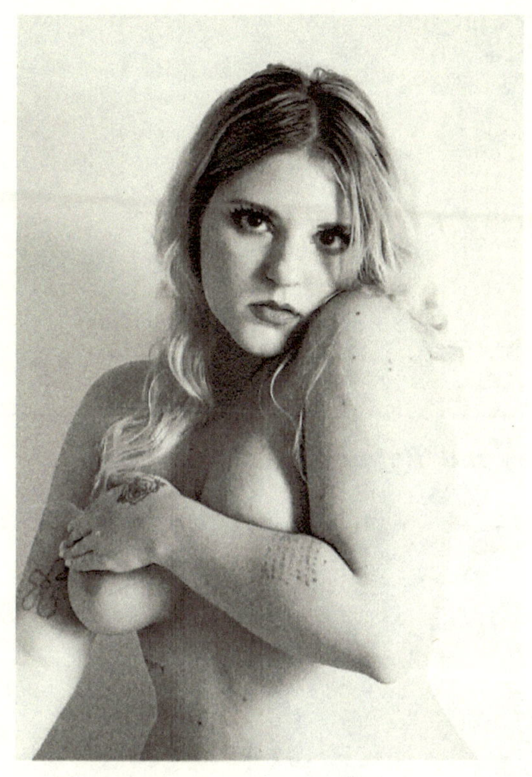

Just-south-of-Dallas native Scarlett Gray (she/they) is a poet, sex worker, and visual artist whose work focuses on raw and gritty personal thoughts and stories all wrapped up in a pretty, albeit-tattered, bow. A huge proponent of talking about the harsh realities of personhood we've been conditioned not to talk about, Scarlett tries not to flinch while working through their damages and secrets in front of an audience.

Venus Reborn is Gray's second full-length book of poetry, following their debut release *Beyond Repair* in 2017.

also available from Scarlett Gray:

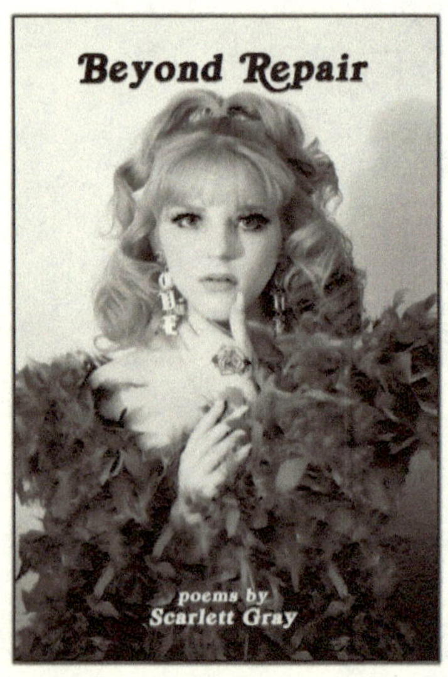

Beyond Repair (2017)

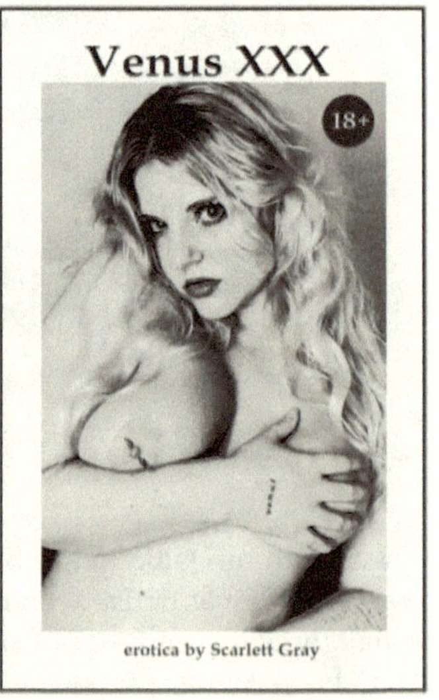

Venus XXX (2020)

www.ingramcontent.com/pod-product-compliance
Lightning Source LLC
LaVergne TN
LVHW090951080826
845145LV00003B/971

* 9 7 8 0 5 7 8 6 4 6 7 8 7 *